AROUND THE DINING TABLE

An Asian-Inspired
Modern Feast

LACE ZHANG

Marshall Cavendish
Cuisine

Editor: Lo Yi Min
Designer: Lynn Chin
All photographs by Lace Zhang, except cover image and those on pages 3 and 6 by
Matthias Chong; image on page 135 by Caecilia, and image on page 152 by Zoe Pei
Food styling for page 67 by Bryan Lim, and pages 105 and 148 by Sandra Sim

Published by Marshall Cavendish Cuisine
An imprint of Marshall Cavendish International

A member of the
Times Publishing Group

Limits of Liability/Disclaimer of Warranty: The Author and Publisher of this book have
used their best efforts in preparing this book. The parties make no representation
or warranties with respect to the contents of this book and are not responsible for
the outcome of any recipe in this book. While the parties have reviewed each recipe
carefully, the reader may not always achieve the results desired due to variations in
ingredients, cooking temperatures and individual cooking abilities. The parties shall
in no event be liable for any loss of profit or any other commercial damage, including
but not limited to special, incidental, consequential, or other damages.

Other Marshall Cavendish Offices:
Marshall Cavendish Corporation, 800 Westchester Ave, Suite N-641, Rye Brook,
NY 10573, USA • Marshall Cavendish International (Thailand) Co Ltd, 253 Asoke,
16th Floor, Sukhumvit 21 Road, Klongtoey Nua, Wattana, Bangkok 10110, Thailand
• Marshall Cavendish (Malaysia) Sdn Bhd, Times Subang, Lot 46, Subang Hi-Tech
Industrial Park, Batu Tiga, 40000 Shah Alam, Selangor Darul Ehsan, Malaysia

National Library Board, Singapore Cataloguing in Publication Data

Name(s): Zhang, Lace.
Title: Around the dining table : an Asian-inspired modern feast / Lace Zhang.
Description: Singapore : Marshall Cavendish Cuisine, [2020]
Identifier(s): OCN 1141440059 | ISBN 978-981-48-6894-5 (paperback)
Subject(s): LCSH: Cooking, Asian
Classification: DDC 641.595--dc23

Printed in Singapore

To my parents,
Dennis and Rhanda

CONTENTS

ACKNOWLEDGEMENTS

This book is made possible only because of the generous support and contributions from so many amazing, giving people that I am lucky enough to have around me.

Joanne and Cuong, thanks for taking the time and effort to host me at the Red Boat Factory on Phu Quoc Island. I am so blessed to have been allowed a sneak peek into the production process, and to have roamed around the breezy island and be treated to many homemade meals and inspiring stories right where the magic happens. Cuong, you are a superhero for bringing Red Boat into existence and taking us to the best food spots in Vietnam. Unforgettable.

Joanne, Karina and Lai Shi Fu, thanks for taking me around Hong Kong and allowing me to *masak-masak* in Shi Fu's kitchen right in the busy Central district of bustling HK. I'm grateful for the memories and the exchange of stories, which involved the patient translation of Shi Fu's words so that I could understand and partake in the conversation.

Sandra (@SandraSim on IG): super thankful you let me shoot at your beautifully lush, self-designed apartment — not once, not twice, but three times — and feeding us all at the shoot with your home-cooked meals, including that insanely fat omelette filled with hand-picked crabmeat. Your HK baked pork chop rice is easily one of the best things ever! Thank you for contributing the recipe, and for sharing your expertise and gorgeous cutlery collection in styling your dish, the tom yum spaghetti and coconut panna cotta.

Caecilia (@singaporeliciouz on IG), Sam and Tish Boyle, thank you for being game to contribute your treasured recipes to this book when I asked! You are such amazing chefs in the kitchen and this book is made even more delicious because of you guys.

Bryan Lim (@bryxnlm on IG), my professional photographer friend, for meticulously styling the pork belly braised in coconut water. Matthias (@mttychng on IG), for shooting the book cover and the shots of me inside this book! Pierre, for listening to me rant on and on about this book and for coming down to the book cover shoot to help out. Without your presence, I wouldn't have known to relax my tense fingers.

Ian, for constantly expanding my horizons.

The team at Marshall Cavendish, thank you all for pulling this book together!

The online community @aroundthediningtable, through which I've been able to meet and interact with so many like-minded, food-obsessed people and fellow home cooks! When I first started this account, never would I have envisioned making so many new friends through it, and the exchange of information, stories and ideas that would ensue. Thanks for letting me talk about snacks, food, recipes and books non-stop without anyone getting seriously bored and wishing I'd shut up. Or if anyone did, I'm blissfully unaware.

Finally, to my mum and dad, thanks for supporting me on this cookbook journey since the start; for helping me get groceries when I was too busy, being my number one recipe taste testers and putting up with the disproportionately large amount of food and photography props in our house.

A FEW WORDS

Since the release of my first book, *Three Dishes One Soup: Inside the Singapore Kitchen*, about two years ago, it's been heart-warming to receive so much support, encouragement and lovely messages! Along the way, I've realised that a lot of the feedback centres on how the recipes are approachable and easy to follow. That they come peppered with little tricks to amp up and max out the flavour without the cook feeling like they've really gone the extra mile. (Hey, the sanity of the cook matters!) A win-win, isn't it? It is in this spirit that I bring forth this new baby, a book full of modern, Asian-inspired recipes for home cooks to play around and experiment with.

I'm unapologetic about taking a more relaxed approach in the kitchen. If your butcher can hack that chicken for you into pieces, or if you'd like to sneak in a shortcut or two — go for it! After all, isn't the act of just cooking — anything — for someone and feeding them an act of love in itself? When we were young, we had all our meals taken care of and planned for. Now that we've grown up and moved out — some of us have even started our own families — we find the roles reversed. We have to figure out our daily meals or what to feed our families on a regular basis. As I mentioned in the introduction of my first book, a home cooked meal like this is the ultimate luxury.

There are a couple of recipes here like the superior stock or fish congee that take a bit more time on the burner — I'll admit that I don't cook them weekly. But if you've got half a day to spare, let me assure you, the rewards reaped are great. What's even better is that they don't require much action on your part; they just need to be left to simmer on the stove and you can get on with whatever else requires your attention at home. Plus, a large pot of stock can be portioned, frozen and refurbished into many more meals. An investment made for your delicious and convenient future!

This book is largely inspired by the Asian pantry where ingredients abound, with many dishes given a fun, modern twist. #NoRules. This is reflective of the current state of our increasingly digital and global world, where the home cook now has access to a global pantry stockpile. We also get inspiration from the world wide web daily and can access the creativity of someone miles away in a single click. Isn't this exchange of ideas amazing?

Here, for our modern Asian feast, we use smoky fish sauce to marinate our steaks (page 60), add a square of umami-laden kombu to some congee we're making (page 88), and combine some shavings of parmesan cheese and a squeeze of lime over Chinese waxed sausages and scallops (page 42). And for something sweet, we use some Asian preserved plums in a sticky pudding-esque cake (page 138). That's the fun of having a global pantry, isn't it? We get to flex our creative juices, experiment in the kitchen and, most importantly, actually enjoy the process.

For times that require the soothing comfort of the familiar, we have grains of jasmine rice suspended in a seafood stock (page 133), fluffy tomato eggs (page 58), cheesy baked pork chop rice (page 78), and a comforting fish congee (page 91) that tastes like it came out of an esteemed restaurant in Hong Kong.

As home cooks, our kitchen isn't like a restaurant's where the same dishes are churned out several times a day, seven days a week. And let's be frank, these days, we might not even have the energy to cook daily. So this leftover situation is something we know all too well —what on earth shall we do with the rest of the cured ham in the packet, the remaining glass noodles or that half a chunk of radish sitting in the fridge? So while we're dealing with whatever else life throws at us, we're also figuring out what to do with leftovers and what to make for our next meal. To salvage this guilt-inducing situation, I've included a "Continuing the Feast" guide with each recipe, which links you up with other recipes here that also make use of, say, Ingredient X.

As such, this becomes your continuous Asian-inspired modern feast. The recipes and ideas here are merely suggestions meant to stir your imaginations, tingle your taste buds, and tease forth your creativity as you whip up your own meals around your dining table.

From one home cook to another,

Lace

IN THE PANTRY

SAUCES, SEASONING AND OIL

OIL
Unless specified otherwise, I use mostly canola oil in these recipes. Feel free to substitute with another neutral-tasting oil of your preference or dietary requirement.

SALT
The salt used here is fine sea salt. If using any other type of salt, e.g. table salt, which tends to be way saltier, do make the necessary adjustments.

LIGHT SOY SAUCE
Soy sauce is indispensable in any Asian kitchen. Even when the food cupboard is empty or sparse, you will find light soy sauce in the pantry of an Asian home. Just a trickle of it over a simple dish, such as plain rice or a fried egg, elevates it. This is made with soy beans that have been fermented. I recommend testing a few brands to find one you like best. A good light soy sauce should have more complexity than just plain saltiness. There are notes of sweetness and sourness, and not just a straight, harsh and grating saltiness.

DARK SOY SAUCE
This is darker, thicker and sweeter than light soy sauce. Use this to add a tinge of sweetness and to make things look more appetising with a darker, caramelised colour.

FISH SAUCE
This book is basically built on this magical condiment — I'm not joking! A good fish sauce should consist of only anchovies and salt, which are left to ferment in barrels until this amber liquid gold results. Add a dash of it to anything and it will instantly taste better. Magic. In this book, it's used in pretty everything much everything to add a saltiness and a funky note of umami.

SRIRACHA
This now ubiquitous condiment is a pungent sauce with a tart edge to it. Just a squeeze of this can rescue anything bland. You can combine this spicy, punchy sauce with mayonnaise, sour cream or even yoghurt to make a creamy dip. It can also work on its own as a dipping sauce served on the side with any grilled meat or noodle dishes.

NAM PRIK PAO
This is a Thai chilli paste that's sweet, salty and spicy with a sticky jammy consistency. You can find these easily at Thai grocery shops or supermarkets. This is the thing you add to give red tom yum its signature colour. You could also dollop some into quick stir-fries or noodle dishes.

THAI CHILLI FLAKES
These ground up Thai chilli flakes have a rusty red hue to them and come speckled with the lethal seeds of the dried chilli. They are potent: a small sprinkling goes a long way. These can be found easily at Thai supermarkets. Substitute with any chilli flakes that have got substantial heat.

THAI PALM SUGAR
The sap of sugar palm, this is used to sweeten many dishes in South East Asian cooking. It adds a more complex, butterscotch note of sweetness to dishes and is particularly lovely in salad dressings. It comes either as a paste, which dissolves more easily, or as a small light-coloured cake that you shave down with a knife before using. Use in place of regular sugar to sweeten curries, stews, teas and desserts.

DRIED GOODS

DRIED CHINESE MUSHROOMS

There are many varieties and the ones that fetch the highest prices are the Japanese ones with a flower pattern on their caps (*hua gu*). To use, soak them in room temperature water for a couple of hours until they soften. But if you are in a rush, use warm or hot water to hasten the process. The soaking liquid is instant flavour-imbuing stock for your dishes. Nothing goes to waste!

FISH MAW

This is dried fish bladder that comes from large fish such as sturgeon or croaker. It is prized for its gelatinous texture and high collagen content (which purportedly keeps us looking youthful), and soaks up flavours easily. It looks like a flattened golden-yellow pouch, but when deep-fried, it looks like a puffy, ridged tube.

DRIED SCALLOPS

Dried scallops are a prized delicacy and the large Japanese ones can command pretty crazy prices. These are often added to stocks, braises and sauces, and also shredded and fried as a crispy topping for rice.

JINHUA HAM

This is a dry-cured ham produced in Jinhua, a city in eastern China's Zhejiang province. It is an intense, meaty and funky cured meat that lends incredible flavour to your dishes. It is commonly used in superior stocks at fancy Chinese restaurants. Adding a small chunk of this really elevates the flavour of your dishes. If unavailable, substitute with Virginia or Iberico ham.

CHINESE WAXED SAUSAGE (*LUP CHEONG*)

This is a dried pork sausage that is a vibrant pinkish-red hue and dotted with little white specks of fat. If you're squeamish about fat, look for ones with fewer visible white specks. As sugar has been added, it is sweeter than regular fresh sausages and will produce a pleasing caramelised note when seared. Chinese waxed liver sausages are typically made with duck liver and much darker in colour — almost black.

RICE AND NOODLES

RICE

Most of the dishes here make use of fragrant Thai jasmine rice, which has a cooking ratio of 1 cup rice to 1 1/4 cup water. We also use glutinous rice, which has a pearly white appearance and is sticky when cooked. They can be added to congee, toasted and ground into powder to add an elusive nutty flavour to dishes, or simply steamed. Some recipes call for Japanese short grain rice, which is starchier than Thai jasmine rice.

RICE VERMICELLI

These rice noodles are great to have on hand for quick stir-fries. The fresh, thicker and rounder rice vermicelli are typically used in noodle soups. I have tried stir-frying them and find that they don't clump together or break into short strands easily, which is perfect for cooks who don't have much experience with frying noodles. The super thin ones, known as *bee hoon*, are available dried at supermarkets, and they also make a satisfying noodle meal in moments.

FLAT RICE NOODLES

These noodles are flatter than rice vermicelli and usually sold fresh at wet markets. They are also available dried, but will need to be soaked according to package instructions before cooking. These days, a variety of dried flat rice noodles can be found — made with brown or black rice, or even tinted golden from turmeric. Slurp these noodles up in broths or wok-fry them for beautiful charring.

GLASS NOODLES (CELLOPHANE NOODLES)

Typically made from mung bean starch or sweet potato starch, these noodles are sold dried and they transform into glassy, silky strands when cooked. These are so tasty because of their ability to soak up flavourful broths yet keep their slight bite. Experiment and find a brand you like. The good ones don't disintegrate easily when cooked. Before using, soak in water for 10–15 minutes.

FRESH AROMATICS

CHILLI

In most dishes that require a substantial kick of heat, I use bird's eye chillies. For a milder level of spiciness, use large red chillies. Experiment with whatever varieties of chilli you happen to have around you, take note of their spice levels and adjust your dishes accordingly!

CILANTRO ROOT

The roots of the cilantro are where most of their flavour is concentrated. You can use them whole in stocks and stir-fries, or pound them into a paste. Before using, rinse them thoroughly to remove any grit that may reside in the nooks, dry and smash lightly with the back of a knife.

KAFFIR LIME LEAF

This leaf is a majestic shade of deep green on one side and a paler shade on the other. Its stem has prickly thorns, so be careful when handling it! Adding this lends an intense citrusy fragrance to your dishes. To use, tear or scrunch up the leaves to help release their aroma.

LIMES

In this collection of recipes, you will find that lime or calamansi lime is the citrus of choice to brighten up many dishes. The larger limes are sharper and more acidic, while the tiny calamansi limes are sweeter, with a more intense and complex citrusy fragrance. As limes vary in the level of tartness and juiciness for each variety and batch, always taste the dish and adjust the seasoning accordingly.

LEMONGRASS

The scent of lemongrass is so soothing and refreshing. To use lemongrass, remove the tough outer leaves and bottom end. The stalk's bottom half is stronger in flavour and thus used in tom yum or marinades. Before adding to stocks or soups, bruise the lemongrass using the back of a knife or a pestle. The more delicately flavoured top halves can be saved for brewing tea or infusing in stocks.

GALANGAL

Whenever I smell galangal, I think of a damp rainforest after a huge downpour because it's got a cooling, piney scent. This is sliced and infused in tom yum soup, and used sparingly in spice or curry pastes.

GINGER

Old or young ginger, it's up to you. The old ones are more fibrous and rough in texture while the young ones are smoother and milder. If you're a ginger fiend and love the spicy kick, go for old.

GINGER TORCH FLOWER

In a beautiful shade of pink and with a regal look to them, these flowers add a refreshing floral and citrusy fragrance to many South East Asian dishes. The petals are tough, with a slight sour finish, but when sliced thinly and used with other herbs or on top of a rich curry, they lift the dish in the most glorious way. You could also halve or quarter the flowers and infuse them in stews. These can be found at wet markets in South East Asia.

GREEN MANGO

If you can get your hands on Thai green mangoes, especially the baby ones, do! They smell so intensely fragrant and refreshing — just peeling their skin releases a tart, fruity fragrance. You can eat their delicious flesh with a sprinkle of plum powder or a chilli-fish sauce dip, or turn them into salads. If these are unavailable, substitute with green papayas or other unripe green mangoes and adjust your dressing to taste.

TURMERIC

Fresh turmeric may resemble ginger on the outside, but once it's sliced, you'll know it's a completely different animal with its intensely orange interior. It has a unique spicy aroma, and will tint *everything* it touches a bright yellow. Turmeric is also available dried and ground into a powder.

WEIGHTS & MEASURES

Quantities for this book are given in Metric, Imperial and American (spoon) measures. Standard spoon and cup measurements used are: 1 tsp = 5 ml, 1 Tbsp = 15 ml, 1 cup = 250 ml. All measures are level unless otherwise stated.

Liquid and Volume Measures

Metric	Imperial	American
5 ml	$^1/_6$ fl oz	1 teaspoon
10 ml	$^1/_3$ fl oz	1 dessertspoon
15 ml	$^1/_2$ fl oz	1 tablespoon
60 ml	2 fl oz	$^1/_4$ cup (4 tablespoons)
85 ml	$2^1/_2$ fl oz	$^1/_3$ cup
90 ml	3 fl oz	$^3/_8$ cup (6 tablespoons)
125 ml	4 fl oz	$^1/_2$ cup
180 ml	6 fl oz	$^3/_4$ cup
250 ml	8 fl oz	1 cup
300 ml	10 fl oz ($^1/_2$ pint)	$1^1/_4$ cups
375 ml	12 fl oz	$1^1/_2$ cups
435 ml	14 fl oz	$1^3/_4$ cups
500 ml	16 fl oz	2 cups
625 ml	20 fl oz (1 pint)	$2^1/_2$ cups
750 ml	24 fl oz ($1^1/_5$ pints)	3 cups
1 litre	32 fl oz ($1^3/_5$ pints)	4 cups
1.25 litres	40 fl oz (2 pints)	5 cups
1.5 litres	48 fl oz ($2^2/_5$ pints)	6 cups
2.5 litres	80 fl oz (4 pints)	10 cups

Dry Measures

Metric	Imperial
30 grams	1 ounce
45 grams	$1^1/_2$ ounces
55 grams	2 ounces
70 grams	$2^1/_2$ ounces
85 grams	3 ounces
100 grams	$3^1/_2$ ounces
110 grams	4 ounces
125 grams	$4^1/_2$ ounces
140 grams	5 ounces
280 grams	10 ounces
450 grams	16 ounces (1 pound)
500 grams	1 pound, $1^1/_2$ ounces
700 grams	$1^1/_2$ pounds
800 grams	$1^3/_4$ pounds
1 kilogram	2 pounds, 3 ounces
1.5 kilograms	3 pounds, $4^1/_2$ ounces
2 kilograms	4 pounds, 6 ounces

Oven Temperature

	°C	°F	Gas Regulo
Very slow	120	250	1
Slow	150	300	2
Moderately slow	160	325	3
Moderate	180	350	4
Moderately hot	190/200	370/400	5/6
Hot	210/220	410/440	6/7
Very hot	230	450	8
Super hot	250/290	475/550	9/10

Length

Metric	Imperial
0.5 cm	$^1/_4$ inch
1 cm	$^1/_2$ inch
1.5 cm	$^3/_4$ inch
2.5 cm	1 inch

MOSTLY GREENS

"One of the very nicest things about life is the way we must regularly stop whatever it is we are doing and devote our attention to eating."

– LUCIANO PAVAROTTI

FRESH SALAD ROLLS WITH PRAWN AND AVOCADO

Tons of fresh herbs and greens are nestled in lightly moistened rice paper, rolled up with some prawns and avocado, and then dipped in this bright, citrusy sauce. It's like a portable salad burrito (kinda). The lemongrass dipping sauce contains three types of citrus fruits, which lend a unique blend of tart-sweetness. My favourite way to serve this is SUPER chilled. Cover the rolls with cling film and stash them in the fridge for a couple of hours to get them chilled to the core. It's the perfect (and healthy) treat for a scorching hot day.

MAKES 6–8 ROLLS

8–10 prawns

A bunch of fresh herbs (basil, cilantro, mint, etc. – I used basil and mint here.)

100 g assortment of vegetables (lettuce, carrot matchsticks, red pepper — anything you fancy. I've kept things simple here with just some lettuce.)

1 avocado

6–8 sheets rice paper rounds

THREE-CITRUS LEMONGRASS DIPPING SAUCE

2 stalks lemongrass, bottom halves only, minced

1 bird's eye chilli, finely minced

2 Tbsp fish sauce

1 1/2 Tbsp white sugar

1 1/2 Tbsp water

2 Tbsp orange juice

2 Tbsp calamansi juice

1 Tbsp lime juice

Continuing the Feast
Avocado is used in Forbidden Rice Grain Bowl (p 72).

Let's start by prepping the dipping sauce. For that, combine the lemongrass, chilli, fish sauce, white sugar, water and citrus juices. Let them hang out while you get on with making your rolls.

Poach the prawns briefly in a pot of boiling water. When they turn pink and curl up, immediately switch off the heat and transfer them to a bowl of iced water. I like soaking prawns this way to ensure they have a bouncy texture.

Prep your herbs and veggies by washing and drying them, then laying them all out on a wide plate.

Peel and core the avocado, then slice it into thin strips. Set this aside too.

Fill a tiny bowl with water. Place a large round plate in front of you and lay out a sheet of rice paper. Moisten the entire surface of the rice paper on both sides by dipping your fingers into the water and running them slowly over the sheet. Do this carefully, ensuring the rice paper is about 80 per cent moistened and not too wet, or it'll become too tacky to handle. You'll get the hang of it after a while.

With the rougher side of the sheet facing up, place a prawn horizontally near the top centre of the sheet. This lets the prawn peek through the translucent rice sheet when it's rolled up. Add a slice of avocado, then pile on the herbs and veggies.

Fold the left and right flaps of the sheet in towards the centre. Slowly, start rolling downwards from the side further from you. Since the rice paper is moistened, gently press the open edges against the roll to seal it. That's one roll done. Repeat until all your ingredients are used up.

Cover with cling film and chill in the refrigerator for about an hour or more if you have the patience and time. Serve chilled with the dipping sauce. You'll never go back to store-bought rolls.

MANGO SALAD WITH PRAWNS

In Hoi An, one of the most memorable dishes I had was a green mango salad. The shreds of fruit were spruced up with a refreshing calamansi dressing, tons of fresh herbs and shards of crisp prawn crackers. These airy crackers add textural dimension to the salad and when dipped lightly in the dressing, they act as the most ethereal, fleeting flavour-delivery vehicle as they dissolve on your palate. To shred the mango, you can use a mandoline, a food processor with a shredding blade or julienne it with your knife. My favourite way to get these shreds is to use this peeler-grater contraption I discovered at one of the morning markets in Vietnam. I simply run the scalloped edges against the fruit and out strews perfectly julienned slices.

SERVES 2 AS A STARTER OR 1 AS A SALAD-ISH MEAL

8–10 prawns, peeled

1 green mango, about 700 g

A bunch of cilantro and mint

Prawn crackers for serving

2–3 Tbsp peanuts for garnishing, roughly chopped

Crispy fried shallots for garnishing

DRESSING

2 Tbsp white sugar

2 Tbsp fish sauce

3 Tbsp calamansi juice

1 small red chilli, finely minced

Continuing the Feast
Green mango is used in Asian Slaw (p 28).

First, make the dressing by mixing the sugar, fish sauce, calamansi juice and red chilli together. Set aside.

Poach the prawns briefly in a pot of boiling water. When they turn pink and curl, immediately switch off the heat and transfer to a bowl of iced water. I like soaking prawns this way to ensure they have a bouncy texture.

Peel and shred the mango using a mandoline, a food processor with the shredding attachment or go old school with just your knife and cutting board.

Dip a few slivers of mango into the dressing to taste. Adjust the seasoning to account for the level of tartness in the mango you use. Taste and make sure you're happy with the end result.

To assemble, toss the mango, dressing and fresh herbs together. Pile onto serving plates, then arrange the prawns and prawn crackers on the side of the salad. Scatter crispy fried shallots and peanuts over. Enjoy!

WOK-CHARRED SPROUTS, THAI STYLE

The best way to cook brussels sprouts is using a wok. Period. That's a scientific fact (maybe) and a life-changing way to deal with this much-maligned veg. Wokking these sprouts serves two purposes: first, to get this incredible char on them as they sear; and second, to control the glazing action that goes on with these babies. What you end up with are these sprouts with perfectly seared edges, glazed beautifully with a sweet, spicy, salty and sour sauce clinging onto their edges. Add some toasted chopped peanuts for a textural contrast and it all pops in your mouth.

SERVES 2–4 AS A SIDE DISH

250 g brussels sprouts

1 clove garlic, peeled

$^{1}/_{2}$–1 small red chilli or
  bird's eye chilli

1$^{1}/_{2}$ Tbsp Thai palm sugar

1 Tbsp fish sauce

1$^{1}/_{2}$ Tbsp canola oil

2 Tbsp peanuts

4 Tbsp water

1 Tbsp lime juice

Lime wedges for garnishing

Continuing the Feast

Thai palm sugar is used in Asian Slaw (p 28), Salmon Belly on a Bed of Herbs (p 48), Thai Steak Salad (p 60), Pork Belly Stew (p 66) and Rice Porridge with Caramel Pork (p 86).

To prep the brussels sprouts, trim and discard their woody ends and halve each little sprout.

Now, for the aromatics and seasoning for this dish. Using a mortar and pestle, mush up the garlic and chilli. Alternatively, use a knife to mince them up. In another bowl, mix together the palm sugar and fish sauce.

Heat a wok over medium-high heat and add in oil. When the oil is hot enough, add the peanuts and fry for 15–20 seconds, until they smell fragrant and are slightly darkened. Drain and set aside to cool. Alternatively, just toast your peanuts for 5–8 minutes in an oven preheated to 180°C, until they turn golden.

Add your sprouts to the hot wok and oil, stir-frying them until they're lightly charred, about a minute or so. You want them to develop a nice sear on their surfaces and edges. Add the garlic and chilli to let them release their aromas, which should take about 20–30 seconds.

Add the water to moisten things up and let the sprouts cook through. If things look a little too dry in there, just trickle in more water. Stir in the palm sugar and fish sauce mixture. Let everything bubble and reduce, until the sauce glazes the sprouts and glistens on the surface. Switch off the heat. Drizzle lime juice over and mix well.

Using a knife or a mortar and pestle, crush the cooled peanuts. To serve, transfer the sprouts to your plate and garnish with the crushed peanuts and some wedges of lime.

WOK-FRIED COCONUTTY GREENS

Using extra virgin coconut oil to stir-fry these greens imbues them with a tropical note and, along with the shallots, lends a sweet finish. This simple yet addictive dish could not be easier to put together and is one my absolute favourite vegetable stir-fries. I first discovered this combination of shallots, bird's eye chilli and fish sauce at my aunt's house when she cooked some Thai baby *gai lan* with it. As for the oil, I was serving curry for our family dinner one evening and decided to use coconut oil for frying the vegetables to complement the meal. It was such a huge hit! This works well with many greens — leafy amaranth, sturdier *gai lan*, or anything you want, really.

SERVES 2–4 AS A SIDE DISH

300 g greens of your choice (bok choy, *nai bai*, spinach, etc.)

1 1/2 Tbsp extra virgin coconut oil

2 shallots, peeled and sliced into thin rings

1 bird's eye chilli, minced

1–2 tsp fish sauce, or to taste

Prep the greens. This would depend on what greens you've chosen. If they have sturdier stems that you don't wish to consume, slice and discard them.

Heat a wok over high heat. Add the oil and let it coat the wok. When the oil is hot enough, lower the heat to medium.

Add the shallots and chilli, then let them sweat for 10–15 seconds, until their aromas are released.

Now, crank the heat up to high. It's time to add the cleaned greens to the wok. Stir-fry over high heat and season with fish sauce. The vegetables will exude a little bit of liquid and that's your sauce. When the greens are just cooked to your liking, switch off the heat and taste for seasoning. These are delicious, I tell you!

The touch of balsamic vinegar splashed on the greens
at the end heightens all the flavours involved.

FRENCH BEANS AMANDINE WITH SWEET CHYE POH

The touch of balsamic vinegar splashed on the greens at the end heightens all the flavours involved. The sweet *chye poh* and dried seafood become even more intensely sweet and savoury at the same time, while the very light back note of acidity lends a dash of intrigue. Pile the dangerously addictive topping onto the beans before you take each juicy bite! Don't fret about making your own XO sauce — I use store-bought sauce in a pinch. Just read the ingredients on the label to make sure you're getting a high-quality one with tons of dried seafood on the ingredient list.

SERVES 2–4 AS A SIDE DISH

1 Tbsp salted butter

15 g almond flakes

1^1/$_2$ Tbsp canola oil or any other neutral-tasting oil

30 g sweet *chye poh* (preserved radish) chunks

250 g French beans, topped and tailed, ends discarded

A pinch of salt

2 Tbsp XO sauce

2 Tbsp water

1–1^1/$_2$ tsp light soy sauce

^{3}/$_4$–1 tsp balsamic vinegar (depending on how sour-sweet your balsamic is — add and adjust to your liking)

Continuing the Feast

XO sauce is used in XO Scallop Noodles (p 101) and Porridge Kueh Stir-Fry (p 102).

Salted butter is used in Brown Butter Coconut Sugar Madeleines (p 143) and Milk Chocolate Chunk Shortbread (p 144).

We start by making our toasty, nutty almond topping. In a small saucepan, combine the salted butter and almond flakes, toasting over low heat until the almonds become lightly golden. Set aside to cool — we'll use it later on for garnishing.

For now, we get on with our stir-fry. Heat a wok over medium-low heat. Add the oil and sweet *chye poh*. Stir-fry until the *chye poh* is fragrant, about a minute or so. Crank the heat up to high and tip in the French beans, stirring constantly and letting them char slightly. Season with a small pinch of salt and the XO sauce.

Add water to help the beans cook, stirring constantly to prevent scorching. Season with soy sauce and keep on frying until the beans are done to your taste.

When the beans are cooked as desired, switch off the heat and splash in the balsamic vinegar. Here's the point to make any final seasoning adjustments!

To serve, tip the beans out onto a serving plate and scrape the delicious sweet and savoury sauce over them. Scatter the buttery toasted almond flakes on top, and et voilà!

ASIAN SLAW WITH TAMARIND-LIME DRESSING

Shredded green mangoes, crunchy green apples and shards of red cabbage, with tons of finely shredded aromatic herbs tossed in the mix, are all pulled together with a spicy, punchy tamarind-lime dressing. The peanut crumble on top is essential, as it adds a toasty crunch and some sweetness! You can find these crunchy caramel peanut bars easily at traditional Chinese snack shops. For this slaw, I prefer small Thai green mangoes for they are more intensely flavoured than the larger ones. Do bear in mind that the tartness will vary for the green mangoes, limes and even the tamarind, so adjust everything to taste, to suit what you have on hand.

SERVES 2

320 g red cabbage

380 g green mango, peeled

100 g green apple

4 stalks lemongrass

8 kaffir lime leaves

4–8 ginger torch flower petals

TAMARIND-LIME DRESSING

2 Tbsp tamarind paste

2 Tbsp water

60 g Thai palm sugar

4 Tbsp lime juice

4 Tbsp fish sauce

2–4 bird's eye chillies, minced

GARNISHING

Caramel peanut bars for garnishing, crumbled

Crispy fried shallots for garnishing

Continuing the Feast

Green mango is used in Mango Salad with Prawns (p 20).

Tamarind paste is used in Smoky Chicken Soup (p 114).

Thai palm sugar is used in Wok-Charred Sprouts (p 22), Salmon Belly on a Bed of Herbs (p 48), Thai Steak Salad (p 60), Pork Belly Stew (p 66) and Rice Porridge with Caramel Pork (p 86).

The bulk of the recipe is getting all your ingredients into thin slices. To shred or julienne the cabbage, green mangoes and apple, you can use a knife, mandoline or food processor.

For the lemongrass, slice them up as thinly as you can manage.

For the lime leaves, remove the woody centre stem before rolling up each half leaf like a cigar and thinly slicing it. Roll up and slice the ginger torch flower petals in a similar manner.

Now, for our tamarind-lime dressing. Use your clean hands to mash up the tamarind paste in a small bowl. Add the water and mix well. Strain the mixture to get rid of seeds and reserve the resulting tamarind water, about 2 teaspoonfuls.

To the tamarind water, add palm sugar, lime juice, fish sauce and minced chilli. Taste and adjust seasoning. The best way would be to dip some of your slaw ingredients into the dressing to make sure you enjoy the overall feel and taste of it all.

To assemble the salad, toss the slaw ingredients together with the dressing. Transfer onto a serving plate and sprinkle with crumbled peanut candy and fried shallots.

CHARRED CAULIFLOWER STEAK WITH YOGHURT-CILANTRO SAUCE

The cauliflower steaks here are stained yellow from their spice marinade and charred till their edges are caramelised and sweet, their insides flowing with sweet juices. We start them off over the stovetop and finish them in the oven for the perfect texture. They are served with a cooling, pale green yoghurt-cilantro sauce. Any leftover sauce can be refurbished into yet another meal by pairing them with a protein like grilled fish or chicken, or used as a dressing for your salad leaves.

SERVES 3–4

1 head cauliflower

1-2 Tbsp canola oil

MARINADE FOR EACH "STEAK"

1 Tbsp canola oil

2 tsp fish sauce

1 Tbsp ground turmeric

A pinch of dried chilli flakes

YOGHURT-CILANTRO SAUCE

140 g full-fat plain Greek yoghurt

35 g cilantro, leaves and
   tender stems

1 clove garlic, peeled

1/2 tsp fish sauce

1/2 tsp salt, or to taste

1/2 tsp lime juice, or to taste

Ground black pepper to taste

TO SERVE

Flaky sea salt

Freshly ground black pepper

Crispy fried shallots

Cilantro leaves, torn

A squeeze of lime juice

> **Continuing the Feast**
> *Ground turmeric is used in Sam's Chicken Satay (p 54) and Lemongrass-Chilli Chicken (p 57).*

First, you gotta butcher your vegetable steaks. Slice the cauliflower lengthwise into fillets that are 4- to 5-cm thick. Depending on the size of your cauliflower, you will get 3 or 4 steaks. Meanwhile, preheat the oven to 175°C.

Depending on how many steaks you have and want to serve, adjust the quantities of the marinade accordingly. Place the cauliflower steaks on a large plate, drizzle the oil, fish sauce, turmeric and chilli flakes over. Rub the marinade evenly over the cauliflower, making sure you get into all the nooks and crannies.

Heat up a frying pan, preferably a cast-iron one, and add in a tablespoonful of oil. Let it heat up over medium-high heat before gently placing one steak down. You'll hear a wonderful sizzling sound. Let it go on until one side is charred, about 50–60 seconds. Flip and let the other side sear for another minute or so.

If using an oven-proof frying pan, place it in the oven. If not, transfer the steaks to a baking tray. Roast for 20–25 minutes, until the cauliflower is cooked through. It's as simple as that.

While the steaks are roasting in the oven, make the sauce. Simply place everything into a food processor or blender and blitz to get a creamy, pale green sauce. Taste and adjust for seasoning.

Remove steaks from the oven and transfer onto individual plates. While the steaks are hot, sprinkle with sea salt and black pepper. Scatter cilantro leaves and crispy fried shallots over, then add a squeeze of lime juice. Serve with yoghurt-cilantro sauce. Devour.

SURF, TURF AND MORE

" *The pleasures of the table belong to all times and ages, to every country and every day; they go hand in hand with all our other pleasures, outlast them, and remain to console us for their loss.* "

– JEAN ANTHELME BRILLAT-SAVARIN

PRAWNS in COCONUT WATER

During dinner in Ho Chi Minh City one night, I came across this dish of shell-on prawns poached ever so gently in coconut water alongside some slices of ginger. It was light, delicate and sweet — nothing too heavy or in your face — and everyone at the table was blown away by the dish. The coconut water really enhances the inherent sweetness of the prawns and the resulting juices act as a dipping sauce for your seafood. Since there's really not much to this dish, get your hands on the best quality coconut water you can find — preferably from freshly cracked coconuts.

SERVES 2–4 AS A SIDE DISH

16–20 prawns

180 ml coconut water

40 g ginger, peeled, chopped into chunks and bruised

¹/₂ tsp salt

Snip off the prawn feelers and any sharp edges of the shell. If you want to, you can devein the prawns by making a slit down the back of their shells and removing the black vein. Wash thoroughly and set them aside in a steaming bowl or shallow dish. Make sure the dish is able to contain the coconut water without overflowing.

Add the coconut water, ginger chunks and salt to the prawns.

Steam over high heat for 3¹/₂–4 minutes, depending on the size of your prawns, until they are tenderly cooked through.

Enjoy the prawns with their coconut broth.

COCONUT WATER RICE

Jasmine rice cooked this way is particularly lovely. The sweet nuttiness of the coconut water pairs well with the aromatic rice grains. This is a nice twist to plain rice, and it echoes the subtle coconut flavours in dishes like the pork belly stewed in coconut water and the steamed prawns above. Try serving this in place of regular white rice next time for a change! If you're scaling the recipe up or down, just stick to the ratio of 1 cup rice to 1¹/₄ cups coconut water.

SERVES 4

400 g Thai jasmine rice, rinsed

500 ml coconut water

Place rice and coconut water in a rice cooker. Use the usual setting for cooking white rice.

When rice is done, fluff it up with a rice paddle and serve.

Continuing the Feast
Coconut water is used in Pork Belly Stew (p 66).

THE ULTIMATE PRAWN TOAST

Is there anything better than deep-fried bread? When you deep-fry white bread, it becomes crispy and filled with large airy pockets. Bless. Here's the ultimate prawn toast so that you have an excuse to consume deep-fried bread. The prawn paste topping is bouncy, crunchy and so flavourful. You can achieve this by the way you work the paste (similar to how the filling is made for wontons) and by sneaking a little lard into it. Each slice of bread is then heaped with an outrageously generous mound of prawn paste, before being smothered in aromatic sesame seeds. When they're deep-frying, you will know they're just about done because you will smell how fragrant they get. Please don't use any fancy bread here – stale white bread is perfect for this.

SERVES 2– 4 AS A SNACK, DEPENDING ON
  HOW LIGHT A SNACKER YOU ARE

2 slices white bread, slightly stale

2–3 Tbsp white sesame seeds

Canola oil for deep-frying

PRAWN PASTE FILLING

200 g prawn meat

15 g lard (optional, but good)

2 stalks spring onions, minced

1/2 tsp salt

Ground white pepper to taste

1/2–3/4 tsp light soy sauce,
  or to taste

1 tsp Shaoxing wine

1 tsp sesame oil

1 tsp cornstarch

1 egg white

Devein the prawns by making a slit down their backs and removing the black vein. Wash and pat dry with paper towels.

Using the flat side of your knife, press down against the prawns and smash them so that they are flattened. Then, you'll want to hack at the meat until it becomes paste-like. Start chopping diagonally in one direction, then going in the other. It's a very natural and easy move to do, much quicker than, say, getting clear cuts of tiny prawn meat. Set aside in a large mixing bowl.

Finely mince the lard and add it to the prawn paste.

To that, add in the spring onions, salt, pepper, soy sauce, Shaoxing wine, sesame oil, cornstarch and egg white. Using clean hands or a pair of chopsticks, keep stirring the mixture until it lightens and becomes tacky. You'll feel the texture change as it becomes a more cohesive mass.

When you are able to handle the sticky mass like a ball, pick it up and slam it hard against the bowl. Do this 10–12 times to ensure a pleasantly bouncy texture for your prawn toast.

Cut the crusts off the bread. Spread the paste equally on the two bread slices, then cover with sesame seeds. Cut each slice of bread into 4 triangles or squares.

Get ready to fry your prawn toast. Add sufficient oil into your cooking vessel of choice and allow it to heat up. You can check if the oil is ready by dipping a large wooden chopstick or spatula into the oil. There should be light bubbles forming around it. If it bubbles too vigorously, reduce the heat.

When the oil is hot, add your bread pieces with the paste side down. When the paste side is nicely golden and puffed up, use a pair of tongs to flip the bread and fry the other side as well. You'll know it's done when you can smell the aroma and the bread pieces are a beautiful golden colour. Drain the toast on paper towels while you fry the remaining pieces.

Plate up and serve alongside any chilli sauce you desire.

GRILLED FISH with BLACK BEAN BROWN BUTTER

I came across black bean brown butter while reading *Top Chef* alum Dale Talde's cookbook, where he basically fused the best of East and West. Funky, salty fermented black beans, meet your new best friend, hazelnutty browned butter. This butter-bean mixture is used to baste the fish — that is, repeatedly spooning the butter over the fish as it cooks in a slightly tilted saucepan. A spritz of citrus juice and zest at the end provides a jolt of brightness to all the earthy richness. Here, I've simply roasted up some baby Chinese broccoli (*gai lan*) to go with the fish, but feel free to use any vegetables, roasted or blanched, or simply some raw salad leaves.

SERVES 2

80 g baby Chinese broccoli (*gai lan*), or broccoli, kale, or greens of your choice

1–2 Tbsp extra virgin olive oil

Sea salt to taste

2 white fish fillets, about 150 g each (any white fish, such as snapper, grouper or bass, is fine)

Ground black pepper to taste

2 Tbsp canola oil

Orange zest for garnishing

Spring onions for garnishing, chopped (optional)

Red chillies for garnishing, sliced (optional)

Lemon or lime wedges to serve

BLACK BEAN BROWN BUTTER

1 clove garlic, peeled and minced

1 shallot, peeled and minced

1/2 tsp minced ginger

Red chillies to taste, minced

1 tsp orange zest

2 tsp preserved black beans in chilli oil

1 tsp light soy sauce

1/4 tsp salt

1/4 tsp white sugar

50 g unsalted butter

Start by making the black bean brown butter. First, place the aromatics — the garlic, shallot, ginger, chillies, orange zest and black beans — and soy sauce, salt and sugar in a heatproof bowl. Then, in a small saucepan, melt butter over low heat, stirring constantly, until the milk solids turn brown. It will smell like the loveliest, nutty liquid ever and turn the colour of roasted hazelnuts. Be careful, we want browned, not burnt, butter. (Been there, done that.)

When it smells right and is amber in colour, immediately pour butter over the aromatics, which will sizzle and soften in the fatty heat. Set aside. You could, at this point, store the butter in the refrigerator for future uses.

Preheat the oven to 220°C. Prep the baby Chinese broccoli by tossing them in 1–2 tablespoonfuls of olive oil. Arrange on a tray and roast for 5–6 minutes. While they're just out of the oven, sprinkle with some flaky sea salt to taste. Set them aside.

For the fish, you'll want the fillets to be absolutely dry. Get them as dry as you possibly can by patting them with paper towels. This will give a nice sear on your fish. Right before searing, season both sides with salt and pepper. Heat a pan over high heat and add the canola oil. When the pan is very hot, use a pair of tongs to place in fillets with skin side down. Don't move or touch them — let the fillets sear and develop that beautiful golden crust.

When the fish is about three-quarters cooked through from the bottom (you can tell as it starts to turn opaque from the bottom up), flip to sear the other side. Add the butter to the pan and continuously spoon it over the fish to finish cooking. Switch off the heat.

To serve, pile some roasted baby Chinese broccoli on your plate and place the fish on top. Grate some orange zest over, then sprinkle with spring onions and chillies, if you have them. Serve with wedges of lime or lemon — this is NOT optional!

SEARED SNAPPER IN HOT AND SOUR BROTH

Like the overlooked girl next door, this clear and delicate style of tom yum soup is usually overshadowed by the exhilarating red-hot tom yum goong, which may even come with an enticing creamy glint. This soup may appear more subdued on the surface but it is by no means any less exciting. In fact, because it doesn't get muddied by any other punchy flavours, its aromatics have a chance to shine through even more. I've provided an option for making your own fish stock here, but you can use a clear chicken stock as well. Instead of poaching fish slices, I've also opted to sear fillets until they're golden brown and have them perched atop this light and flavourful broth.

SERVES 2

500 ml fish stock (see method) or seafood stock (p 133)

2 stalks lemongrass, outer layers removed, bottom halves bruised and cut into smaller chunks, top halves reserved for fish stock

5 kaffir lime leaves, torn and scrunched up

8 slices galangal, peeled

3–4 Thai chillies, the tiny ones, thickly sliced

125 g baby corn, chopped into thirds

150 g oyster mushrooms

8–10 cherry tomatoes, halved

2–2 1/2 Tbsp fish sauce, or to taste

1 1/2 tsp white sugar

3 Tbsp lime juice, or to taste

2 red snapper (or sea bass or grouper) fillets

Canola oil for frying

Cilantro leaves for garnishing

FISH STOCK

150 g fish bones

1.2 litres water

1 onion, peeled and quartered

1 cilantro root

Tops of 2 stalks lemongrass (see above)

2 stalks spring onions (optional)

To make the fish stock, place all the ingredients in a large pot. Bring to a gentle boil and let simmer for about 20 minutes. Remove from heat and strain stock. You won't need the full amount unless you're preparing enough to serve 4 people. You can save the excess stock for other dishes: it can be kept frozen for up to 2 months or refrigerated for 1–2 days .

To make the soup, infuse the fish stock with all the aromatics — the lemongrass, lime leaves, galangal, chillies — over low heat for 5–10 minutes, then add your baby corn and oyster mushrooms to let them cook through, about 5 minutes. Season with fish sauce by adding 2 tablespoonfuls first and working your way up if you want a saltier soup. Add the sugar and lime juice, then taste and adjust with more lime juice or chillies to your liking. Finally, toss in the cherry tomatoes and switch off the heat

Set the soup aside while you sear the snapper. Score each fillet on its skin side by making two tiny incisions in the centre. Be careful not to cut all the way through. Season both sides with salt and black pepper. Heat a pan over medium heat until smoking hot, then drizzle in some oil to coat its surface. When the pan is very hot, place in fillets with skin side down. When the fish is about three-quarters cooked, flip fillets over to lightly sear the other side.

Ladle the tom yum soup, along with its aromatics and ingredients, into a shallow bowl. Top with the seared snapper, with its skin side up. Garnish with cilantro if desired and serve to your lucky guests.

Continuing the Feast

Galangal is used in Laab Meatballs (p 64), Tom Yum Spaghetti (p 104), Creamy Tom Yum Goong (p 112), Vegetarian Pho (p 118) and Vegan Tom Yum (p 130).

Cilantro root is used in Peppery Glass Noodles (p 108).

SEARED SCALLOPS OVER CORN AND LUP CHEONG

This is one of my favourite dishes in this book as it hits all the right flavour spots. Just think: Juicy, smoky chunks of sweet corn kernels interspersed with salty-sweet bits of *lup cheong* and shallots, topped with crusty, seared scallops. Lashings of pecorino cheese and the squeeze of lime at the end tie everything together, making the flavours all sing, pop and party in your mouth. People will think you've laboured over the stove when, really, it takes moments of work to make something this beautiful! Go make this. You're welcome.

SERVES 2 AS A STARTER

20 g Chinese waxed sausage
 (*lup cheong*)

1 ear corn, shucked

2 Tbsp extra virgin olive oil

1 shallot, peeled and thinly sliced

4–5 stalks spring onions, green
 and white portions separated,
 both portions chopped

1 tsp light soy sauce

Salt to taste

Ground black pepper to taste

1 Tbsp unsalted butter

6–8 scallops

2 Tbsp canola oil

Grated pecorino cheese to taste
 (or use Parmigiano Reggiano
 or Grana Padano)

Lime wedges to serve

Continuing the Feast

Chinese waxed sausage is used in Waxed Meats Rice (p 77) and Radish Cake (p 82).

Pecorino cheese or Parmigiano-Reggiano can be used in Tom Yum Spaghetti (p 104).

Soak the sausage in water for about 10 minutes and remove its casing. Chop into small chunks about the same size as a corn kernel or slightly larger.

Remove kernels from the corn cob and set aside.

Heat a large saucepan over medium heat and add your olive oil. Reduce the heat to low and add the sausage. Let it cook for a few minutes, allowing the fat to slowly render out as the sausage lightly crisps up. Add the shallot slices and the white portion of the spring onions, letting them slowly caramelise in the sausage fat. It will look and smell heavenly.

When the mixture has taken on some colour, crank the heat up to high as you tip in the corn kernels. Mix and cook for 3–4 minutes until the corn is just cooked through and still crunchy and sweet (don't worry; corn is very forgiving and retains crunch well). Season with soy sauce, and salt and pepper to taste. To finish, stir in the butter to coat the corn. Taste and adjust for seasoning. Set this mixture aside in a bowl while you get on with your scallops.

Pat the scallops dry with paper towels. VERY DRY. This is essential if you want scallops with a golden crust! Season the scallops with salt and pepper on both sides. Heat a pan over high heat and add the canola oil. Allow the oil to heat up — make sure it's very hot! Again, this is crucial for that nice sear.

Then, using a pair of tongs, place your scallops in the pan in a single layer, leaving them to sear over high heat until a beautiful crust develops underneath — about a minute or so. Resist the urge to touch or move them! When you see the edges brown from the side, check the seared side with your tongs. When you're happy with the sear, flip the scallops over to quickly sear them on the other side. Once the other side is browned, immediately remove scallops from the heat to prevent further cooking.

To plate, portion the corn mixture into two serving bowls. Plop your scallops on top, grate some pecorino over and garnish with chopped green portion of spring onions. Serve with lime wedges — this is REALLY NOT optional! Squeeze the lime over and enjoy.

People will think you've laboured over the stove when, really, it takes moments of work to make something this beautiful!

TOFU WITH PORK FLOSS, SHREDDED OMELETTE AND TOBIKO

When I was in Hong Kong, I visited Lai Shi Fu (his radish cake recipe is on page 82), and his daughter, Karina, very generously shared her favourite haunts with me as she took me around for some traditional HK snacks. We passed by a shop selling huge rice rolls — I'm talking burritos made of starchy, sticky rice, compressed like a log around pork floss, eggs and, yes, deep-fried dough fritters. The rolls were secured in cling wrap to keep everything snug. I think pork floss and egg is one of the best food combinations ever, so I've lightened everything up here with silken tofu as the base instead. If you can get a hold of them, use those ultra-creamy, Japanese tofu blocks that are almost custard-like in texture. Treat this recipe more like a guide and use your own instincts and taste buds to work out proportions.

SERVES 2–4

1–2 eggs

A pinch of salt

A pinch of ground white pepper

2 Tbsp canola oil

1–2 blocks silken tofu (the kind that's best suited for eating raw), chilled

Pork floss as desired (I use the crispy kind, but use any kind you prefer, or even chicken floss or fish floss)

30–40 g *tobiko* (flying fish roe), to taste

Spring onions for garnishing, chopped

SAUCE

1 Tbsp light soy sauce

1 tsp chilli oil or sesame oil

1 tsp mirin

Continuing the Feast

Mirin is used in Drunken Eggs (p 51) and can be added to dishes that need a tinge of sweetness, such as soups or stews.

Pork floss can be used to top porridge dishes, like Rice Porridge with Caramel Pork (p 86).

Mix all the sauce ingredients in a bowl and set aside.

In another bowl, beat the eggs with the salt and pepper. If you're making a smaller portion, one egg would suffice. Heat a pan or wok over medium-low heat and add the oil. When the pan is hot, pour in the eggs and fry to make an omelette. As we will be shredding the omelette, you don't have to worry about flipping it perfectly. By all means, cut that thing in half with your spatula to flip it if you wish to. Remove the omelette from the heat. Roll it up and slice into thin strips.

To assemble, place a block of tofu on a serving plate. If you prefer, drizzle some sauce on top of the tofu now, or choose to serve it on the side if you'd rather preserve the pristine whiteness of your tofu. Top with the pork floss generously — make it rain! — followed by omelette strips and *tobiko*. Garnish with spring onions, if desired.

Serve and enjoy the cold, creamy goodness!

STEAMED FISH with TONS OF GARLIC, CHILLIES and LIME

Whenever you're in a seafood-centric eatery in Thailand or Vietnam, there's always the option to have your seafood simply steamed and paired with a garlicky lime juice and fish sauce concoction. The fish usually comes suspended in a saucy broth and served on a metal platter on top of a warmer, the entire fish smothered with tons of chopped garlic, chillies and cilantro. If you find yourself caught in the lucky situation of having leftover sauce, just steam up some prawns, squid or other seafood you desire, and drizzle the sauce over.

SERVES 2

1 whole red snapper or sea bass or red grouper

1 stalk lemongrass, bruised

Cilantro leaves for garnishing

SAUCE

240 ml fish stock or seafood stock or chicken stock

10–12 cloves garlic, peeled and minced

4–6 red chillies, or to taste, minced

75 ml fish sauce

85 ml lime juice

1½ Tbsp white sugar or Thai palm sugar

Continuing the Feast
Fish stock is used in Seared Snapper (p 40).

Seafood stock is used in Seafood Soup with Rice (p 133).

First, clean your fish by running it under tap water and checking that its cavity is clear of any gunk or residue. I usually just get my fishmonger to scale and gut the fish for me — it makes for an easier life in the kitchen.

After your fish is cleaned, score it on both sides with 2 or 3 slashes to allow for even cooking. Place the lemongrass stalk inside the fish, then arrange the fish on a large steaming dish with sides high enough to contain the sauce.

Steam over high heat for 10–12 minutes, depending on the size of your fish. To check if the fish is cooked, pierce its thickest part with a toothpick. If it does not meet with any resistance, the fish is done.

While the fish is steaming, prep your sauce. Simply mix the stock, garlic, chillies, fish sauce, lime juice and sugar. Taste and adjust for seasoning.

Remove the perfectly steamed fish and discard its juices. Pour the sauce over, top with cilantro leaves, and serve immediately with some steamed white rice.

SALMON BELLY ON A BED OF HERBS

Cubes of fatty salmon belly are crisped up in a pan until golden brown and their fatty insides melt when they are in your mouth. As always, a coarse sprinkle of sea salt on the crusty, fatty salmon right after it's cooked lifts the heavy oiliness. Here, it sits on a bed of fresh herbs that are slicked with a Thai chilli jam dressing. As salmon is an oily fish, it is able to stand up to the assertive jam.

SERVES 1

150 g salmon belly, cut into cubes

Salt as needed

Ground black pepper as needed

1 Tbsp canola oil

½ red onion, peeled and thinly sliced

A huge bunch of fresh herbs (mint, basil, cilantro, sawtooth coriander or dill — a mix of any of these would work)

Crispy fried shallots for garnishing (optional)

CHILLI DRESSING

1½ tsp *nam prik pao* (Thai chilli paste)

2 tsp fish sauce

½ tsp Thai palm sugar

2 tsp lime juice, or to taste

2 tsp water

Pat salmon belly cubes dry thoroughly, then season lightly with salt and black pepper.

Heat a pan over medium heat and trickle in the oil. Don't worry if this doesn't seem like enough: the salmon belly's fat will ooze out and add to it. When the oil is hot enough, add your chunks of salmon belly. It should sizzle boldly. Sear salmon on all sides, reducing the heat to prevent any burning before the edges are crispy. Set aside and immediately sprinkle with a pinch of coarse sea salt.

To the hot pan (with the fire switched off), add the onion and let the residual heat soften and wilt it slightly.

Combine all the dressing ingredients in a bowl. Taste and adjust seasoning as desired.

To serve, lay the herbs on a plate and top with the wilted onion. Drizzle some dressing over and arrange salmon cubes on top. Scatter the crispy fried shallots over if using.

Continuing the Feast

Nam prik pao is used in Tom Yum Spaghetti (p 104), Creamy Tom Yum Goong (p 112) and Vegan Tom Yum (p 130).

Thai palm sugar is used in Wok-Charred Sprouts (p 22), Asian Slaw (p 28), Thai Steak Salad (p 60), Pork Belly Stew (p 66) and Rice Porridge with Caramel Pork (p 86).

MARINATED DRUNKEN EGGS

These Shanghai-style marinated eggs come by way of Joycelyn Shu, one of the most meticulous and knowledgeable home cooks I have the pleasure of knowing. She uses them as a topping for her vegetarian pho (p 118), but really, you should just make a big batch, stash it in the fridge for the next couple of days and future you would be grateful you did just that. Stave off hunger pangs any time of the day by consuming this salty-sweet oozy egg, or use it to top just about anything — instant noodles, noodle soups, salads or store-bought meals. I present to you, in true Joycelyn fashion, her incredibly detailed instructions.

MAKES 6 EGGS

3 litres water

6 large eggs

MARINADE

250 ml water

250 ml Shaoxing wine

125 ml light soy sauce

125 ml mirin

100 g raw cane sugar

Continuing the Feast
Mirin is used in Tofu with Pork Floss (p 45) and can be added to dishes that need a tinge of sweetness, such as soups or stews.

The volume of water and number of eggs listed yield a particular texture in the given time frame. If you wish to use more or fewer eggs, please experiment and adjust the timing accordingly.

Bring the water to the boil in a medium pot. Use a wide Chinese mesh skimmer or strainer to carefully lower in the eggs. Immediately turn the heat down so the water reaches a bare simmer; small bubbles should barely break the surface of the water. Cook for $6\,^1/_2$ minutes for a molten yolk with tender, just-set whites, or 7–8 minutes if you prefer a firmer texture.

Meanwhile, get ready a large bowl of iced or very cold water. Once eggs are done to your preferred consistency, transfer to the prepared bowl to arrest cooking and ease the peeling.

Once eggs are cooled, gently crack them all over with a spoon. Peel carefully as the whites will be rather delicate; start peeling from the wider end, which contains the air pocket. Set aside the peeled eggs in a medium bowl which fits them comfortably.

For the marinade, combine all the ingredients and stir until the sugar is dissolved.

Pour the marinade over the eggs until the eggs float and are just covered. To keep the eggs fully submerged and marinating evenly, place two layers of paper towels on top and press down gently until the towels are completely saturated. Place cling film over the bowl, refrigerate, and marinate for at least 12 hours and up to 24 hours. The eggs become firmer and saltier the longer they marinate.

TEA-SMOKED DUCK LEGS

If you've been to Hong Kong, you'd probably know the joys of biting into a mahogany-coloured roasted goose leg. You clutch the bone like you're straight outta *The Flintstones* and sink into that bad boy, its divine fatty juices spurting out, intermingling with the whiff of smoke and seasoning. All very complex, all very bad, but tasting so damn good.

It's not easy to purchase goose where I am, so I smoke and roast up a fatty duck leg instead and yes, it is a many-splendored thing. Don't be alarmed by the sound of tea-smoking something. It merely involves lining your wok with foil, piling on a mixture of rice, tea leaves and sugar, then allowing the duck legs to mingle with them over high heat for 10–15 minutes.

SERVES 2

1 Tbsp Sichuan peppercorns
2 Tbsp flaky sea salt
2 duck legs, about 370 g each
1 Tbsp Chinese rice wine
1 stick cinnamon
1 star anise
2 slices ginger

TEA-SMOKING
3 Tbsp tea leaves
120 g brown sugar
120 g jasmine rice

Continuing the Feast
Cinnamon sticks and star anise are used in Braised Beef Brisket (p 63), Chilli Beef Noodz (p 98) and Vegetarian Pho (p 118).

We start by marinating the duck the night before. Toast the peppercorns in a pan over medium-low heat for about 30 seconds. Transfer to a mortar and pestle, add the sea salt and grind until fine. Rub the salt mixture and Chinese rice wine on the duck legs and leave to marinate overnight.

To steam the duck legs, place them on a large steaming plate, together with the cinnamon, star anise and ginger. If you have a steam oven or a steamer, go ahead and use that. If not, heat some water in a wok that's fitted with a metal steaming rack. Steam the duck legs over low heat for 1.5 hours (or more if you prefer), until the legs are tenderly done to your liking. Set aside.

To smoke the duck, simply line a clean and dry wok with two layers of aluminium foil, making sure its entire bottom and sides are covered. This will allow for an easy clean-up afterwards. Scatter the tea leaves, brown sugar and rice on top, then set the steaming rack over the mixture.

Pat the duck legs dry with paper towels before placing them on the rack. Cover the wok and crank the heat up to high. Smoke the duck legs over high heat for 10 minutes, switch off the heat, then let sit for another 5 minutes inside the wok.

Meanwhile, preheat the oven to 190°C. When the duck legs are done smoking, give them a blast in the oven for 15–20 minutes, until the skin crisps up and the fat is glistening off it.

Serve with steamed rice and a side of good quality store-bought plum sauce. The tart sauce will cut through and complement the duck's fattiness.

It's not easy to purchase goose where I am, so I smoke and roast up a fatty duck leg instead and yes, it is a many-splendored thing.

SAM'S CHICKEN SATAY WITH SPICY CALAMANSI DIP

This is a recipe contributed by my friend Sam Chablani, who makes a career of grilling meats and things over charcoal fire. He helmed Fat Lulu's, a joint that specialised in the art of Asian barbecue, and is the Charcoal King and creator of #noburnnotaste. Sam has very kindly given me a satay recipe that's inspired by the food he had while travelling around the islands between southern Thailand and northern Malaysia. The chicken chunks are kept moist with a) layers of its fat and skin, and b) spoonfuls of coconut oil to lubricate the meat and keep it velvety. The ground turmeric is only added right before grilling or while on the grill. Season the meat with sprinkles of it like you would with salt to keep the flavour bright. If you have access to a charcoal grill during your next cookout, you know what dish you should make.

MAKES 8–10 STICKS

600 g chicken thighs, boneless, skin on

2 Tbsp ground turmeric

MARINADE

1 bird's eye chilli, chopped

2 cloves garlic, peeled and smashed

1 Tbsp honey

1 Tbsp light soy sauce

3 Tbsp extra virgin coconut oil

SPICY CALAMANSI DIP

50 ml calamansi juice

1 red bird's eye chilli, chopped

1 green bird's eye chilli, chopped

1 tsp finely minced lemongrass

1 tsp finely minced kaffir lime leaves

1 Tbsp cilantro leaves, chopped

1 tsp desiccated coconut

Continuing the Feast

Desiccated coconut is used in Thai Steak Salad (p 60) and Coconut Panna Cotta (p 149).

Ground turmeric is used in Charred Cauliflower Steak (p 30) and Lemongrass-Chilli Chicken (p 57).

Cut the chicken into 1.5-cm chunks. Combine all the marinade ingredients and the chicken in a large ziplock bag. Seal and leave to marinate in the refrigerator for at least 4 hours, or better yet, overnight.

While the chicken is marinating, soak 10 wooden skewers in water for a couple of hours.

To thread the marinated chicken, use a couple of chunks per skewer. Make sure that it alternates between meat and skin as you thread.

Right before grilling, sprinkle some ground turmeric over the meat.

Heat the grill, making sure the fire is low to medium. You don't want to go crazy high here or else the sugar in the honey will burn before everything is cooked through. Grill skewered meat on all sides until cooked through and lightly caramelised, with an internal temperature of 75°C (165°F).

You can eat this as is, or serve with the spicy calamansi dip.

To make the dip, combine all the ingredients except the desiccated coconut. Add the desiccated coconut to the dip just before serving the satay.

Then, in Sam's words, "Dip the chicken in the sauce, lean back and be like DAYUMMM!"

GRILLED LEMONGRASS-CHILLI CHICKEN

Don't you just love hearing the spitting sizzle of a promising char as meat hits a hot pan? Then out wafts the aromas that were dormant in the marinade, their true personalities now teased forth by the heat and oil. This killer marinade packs a huge flavour punch from the use of freshly pounded aromatics, and it also tenderises the chicken meat to utter succulence. Since we're using thighs here, there's no need to fuss about the meat getting overcooked or dry. You can use this versatile, reliable recipe in your repertoire for just about anything — from grain bowls to sandwiches, or just for serving up with some quickly sautéed vegetables.

SERVES 2

1 stalk lemongrass

1 garlic, peeled

1 shallot, peeled

1 Tbsp ground turmeric

1 Tbsp sriracha

1¹/₂ tsp fish sauce

1 tsp sesame oil

¹/₄ tsp salt

Ground black pepper to taste

200 g boneless chicken thighs, skin removed

2 Tbsp canola oil or extra virgin coconut oil

Continuing the Feast

This grilled chicken is used in the Forbidden Rice Grain Bowl (p 72) and Bao Mi (p 85).

Ground turmeric is used in Charred Cauliflower Steak (p 30) and Sam's Chicken Satay (p 54).

For the lemongrass, remove the tough outer leaves and use only the tender inner stems of the bottom half. If using a mortar and pestle, pound the aromatics — garlic, shallot and lemongrass — together. If not, individually mince them finely and combine.

Mix the aromatics, turmeric, sriracha, fish sauce, sesame oil, salt and pepper to make the marinade. Massage it onto the chicken thighs and leave to marinate for at least 30 minutes. I sometimes do this the night before so that the marinade's tenderising effect is even stronger and the flavours seeping through are more intense.

When you are ready to cook, heat a grill or a saucepan over medium-high heat and tip in the oil. When the oil is hot, use a pair of tongs to place the chicken in the pan. Reduce the heat to medium-low and let it sear on one side, about 2 minutes. Check that the first side is seared to a golden brown then flip to cook the other side through. Leave to rest for 5–10 minutes before slicing and serving.

TOMATO EGG

To me, the perfect tomato egg has curds that are just set, not runny (we're not doing a Western-style scramble now, are we?), and certainly not a leaky or watery mess! The ratio of tomato to eggs is also key here. Like in any rewarding relationship, they are partners of equal standing, each playing their part to boost the other, neither one outshining or overpowering the other — we don't want a tomato salad coddled with a little egg here.

SERVES 2–4 AS A SIDE DISH

FOR THE EGGS

4 eggs

¼ tsp salt

A dash of white pepper

1 tsp Shaoxing wine

½ tsp cornstarch dissolved in 1 tsp water

1 Tbsp canola oil or corn oil

Spring onions for garnishing, chopped

FOR THE SAUCE

1 tomato

¼ white onion, peeled

60 g ketchup

1 tsp cornstarch, dissolved in 1 Tbsp water

4 tsp water

½ tsp white sugar

½ tsp light soy sauce

1 Tbsp canola oil or corn oil

A pinch of salt

Continuing the Feast
Tomatoes and ketchup are used in Baked Pork Chop Rice (p 78).

Prepare the sauce first. Slice the tomato in half, then cut each half into 2 or 3 large wedges. Slice the onion thinly.

Mix the ketchup, cornstarch slurry, water, sugar and soy sauce in a bowl. Keep this handy.

Heat a wok over medium-high heat and add the oil. When the oil is hot, toss in the onion with a small pinch of salt. Continue stir-frying until onion is softened but not brown. Add the tomato chunks and leave them for about 30 seconds to char. Drizzle in the ketchup mixture and let everything come to the boil. Once the sauce thickens, switch off the heat and set aside in a bowl.

We'll now be cooking the eggs. In a bowl, beat the eggs, salt, pepper, Shaoxing wine and cornstarch slurry together.

Rinse your wok to get rid of any tomato-ey residue, then heat the cleaned wok over medium-low heat. Add the oil and when it is hot, pour in the beaten eggs and, working quickly, use a spatula to draw the sides of the egg mixture towards the centre. You want it to be cooking evenly, so keep doing this until the eggs are 80 per cent done. The wok is hot, so this happens quickly! Switch off the heat and let the eggs cook in the residual heat. Toss in the sauce and mix well.

When the egg curds are just set and marbled red with the sauce, dish out and garnish with spring onions.

THAI STEAK SALAD

The quick and lean Thai-style dressing here perks up all the fresh vegetables and the steak slices that even a vegetable-hater (ahem, my mum) wipes the entire plate clean. The garnish of toasted coconut and crushed peanuts adds a textural crunch and, if you're using the coconut oil to sear the steak, echoes the coconutty flavour. Do note that the dressing will add another layer of seasoning to the dish, so don't over-salt the initial marinade. If you can get your hands on smoky fish sauce that has been aged in bourbon barrels, it is marvelous for splashing on the steaks before you sear them.

SERVES 2

2 rib-eye steaks, about 200–220 g each

¹/₂ stalk lemongrass, the bottom half, minced

4 tsp fish sauce

1 tsp brown sugar

Tons of freshly ground black pepper

2 Tbsp canola oil or coconut oil

Salad leaves of your choice (baby spinach, arugula, romaine, or any mix you want), rinsed and dried

Cherry tomatoes (and any other type of fresh vegetables you like or have on hand)

Desiccated coconut for garnishing, toasted

Peanuts for garnishing, chopped

DRESSING

1¹/₂ Tbsp fish sauce

2 tsp Thai palm sugar (substitute with white sugar or brown sugar)

1¹/₂ Tbsp lime juice

Bird's eye chillies to taste, minced

We start by marinating our steaks. Mix the lemongrass, fish sauce, sugar and pepper together. Rub the marinade onto the steaks and let sit for 10–15 minutes, allowing the flavours to infuse the meat.

Meanwhile, mix all the dressing ingredients together. Dip some salad leaves into the dressing to taste it, then adjust the seasoning to your liking.

To sear the marinated beef, heat a sauté pan over high heat. When the pan is hot, drizzle in the oil and let it heat up. Using a pair of tongs, place the steaks in the pan and let sit until a nice char develops. Flip over to seat the other side and cook until your desired doneness.

Transfer the steaks to a cutting board and leave to rest for 5–10 minutes. Meanwhile, toss the salad leaves and tomatoes in the dressing. Start with a small amount and slowly add more as needed to prevent the salad from being overdressed. Portion onto serving plates.

Slice the steaks and arrange them on top of the vegetables. Drizzle some dressing over the beef and scatter the coconut and peanuts over the salad.

Continuing the Feast

Leftover salad leaves can be used in Laab Meatballs (p 64) and Forbidden Rice Grain Bowl (p 72).

Desiccated coconut is used in Sam's Chicken Satay (p 54) and Coconut Panna Cotta (p 149).

Thai palm sugar is used in Wok-Charred Sprouts (p 22), Asian Slaw (p 28), Salmon Belly on a Bed of Herbs (p 48), Pork Belly Stew (p 66) and Rice Porridge with Caramel Pork (p 86).

BRAISED BEEF BRISKET WITH TENDONS

Timing is key in this recipe, which comes from my dad's sister, Fu Lan Chan. She took many attempts to figure out exactly how long the meat should be braised to achieve the perfect texture — without threatening to disintegrate into a murky mess in your pot, the tendons are gelatinously yielding with a slight bite and the brisket is tender. My aunt's cooking style is precise where it matters and adaptable where creativity is called for. Here, she layers the umami from fermented bean curd, oyster sauce and soy sauce. She also adds a couple of preserved orange peel plums (those that we can eat as a snack), but in the same spirit of flexibility and creativity, I'm encouraging you to use whatever that's easily available to you, be it the fresh zest of oranges or some aged mandarin peel.

SERVES 6–8

1½ Tbsp canola oil or vegetable oil

500 g beef tendons, cut into
  4-cm chunks

Enough water or stock to just
  cover the beef

20 g ginger, peeled and
  crushed lightly

1 star anise

1 stick cinnamon

2 preserved orange peel plums

1.5 kg beef brisket, cut into
  4-cm chunks

1 Tbsp red fermented bean curd

1 Tbsp oyster sauce

1 Tbsp dark soy sauce

1 Tbsp light soy sauce

Salt to taste

Continuing the Feast
Cinnamon sticks and star anise are used in Tea-Smoked Duck Legs (p 52), Chilli Beef Noodz (p 98) and Vegetarian Pho (p 118).

Heat a Dutch oven or pot over high heat and add in the oil. Sear the tendons first until they are lightly golden brown. Add enough water or stock to just cover the tendons. Add the ginger, star anise, cinnamon and orange peel plums.

Let it stew over low heat for 1 hour before adding the brisket. Season with the fermented bean curd, oyster sauce, and dark and light soy sauces.

Leave to braise for another 2 hours, by which time everything will be at optimum doneness. The tendons would have just the right amount of resistance for them to lend a pleasurable bite, and the brisket will be tender, but not overly mushy or falling apart.

Adjust to taste with salt and more light soy sauce. This is best enjoyed spooned over rice or noodles.

DEEP-FRIED LAAB MEATBALLS

You know the famous north-eastern Thai salad of minced meat with herbs, spices and ground toasted rice, usually served in lettuce cups in restaurants? Same same, but deep-fried as meatballs. Just like in a traditional *laab* salad, there's a sour, spicy aromatic kick to this meatball. For added texture and aroma, glutinous rice is toasted in a pan with some kaffir lime leaves before it's ground up and added to the meatball mixture. The acidity from the lime juice and the shallots also work to tenderise the meat, so you'll get juicy meatballs with a deliciously golden crust.

MAKES 16–20 MEATBALLS

3 Tbsp (45 g) short grain white glutinous rice

2 kaffir lime leaves, finely sliced

2 stalks lemongrass

5–6 shallots, peeled and minced

2 tsp galangal, peeled and minced

400 g minced pork (make sure it's as fatty as you can stomach)

2 Tbsp fish sauce

3–4 Tbsp lime juice

1–2 tsp chilli flakes, or to taste

1 tsp white sugar

Cilantro to taste, chopped

Canola oil or sunflower oil or peanut oil for deep-frying

Lime wedges for garnishing

Mint leaves for garnishing

Salad leaves for serving

Continuing the Feast

Glutinous rice is used in Fish Congee (p 91).

Galangal is used in Seared Snapper (p 40), Tom Yum Spaghetti (p 104), Creamy Tom Yum Goong (p 112), Vegetarian Pho (p 118) and Vegan Tom Yum (p 130).

Leftover salad leaves can be used in Thai Steak Salad (p 60) and Forbidden Rice Grain Bowl (p 72).

Make the toasted rice powder. Heat the glutinous rice and lime leaves in a dry pan over medium-low heat. Stir constantly to ensure even heat distribution, and cook until the grains smell nutty and are golden brown. Remove from heat and set aside.

For the lemongrass, remove the tough outer leaves and use only the tender inner stems of the bottom half. (You can save the tops parts to make tea.) If using a mortar and pestle, pound the aromatics — lemongrass, shallots and galangal — together. If not, individually mince them finely and combine.

Combine the minced aromatics with the pork. Season with the fish sauce, lime juice, chilli flakes and sugar. Add the chopped cilantro — unless you hate cilantro. Set aside to marinate.

Return to the cooled rice and lime leaves. Transfer the rice to a food processor, blender or mortar and pestle to grind into a powder. The mixture doesn't have to be completely powdered — leaving some nubs will add interesting texture.

Add the rice powder to the pork mixture. Mix until everything comes together. You can microwave or fry a little of the meatball to check for seasoning. Adjust with more fish sauce, lime juice or chilli flakes to taste.

Divide into 16–20 portions and form a ball with each portion.

To deep-fry the meatballs, heat a generous amount of oil in a wok or pot. If you have a deep-fry thermometer, let the oil reach 175–180°C. If, like me, you are not using one, just say a prayer and use your intuition. You can gauge when the oil is hot enough by dipping a wooden chopstick or spatula into the oil. There should be bubbles rising around the stick, neither too vigorously nor too lazily. Don't worry, you'll get the hang of it after a few batches.

When your oil is ready, add a few meatballs to the wok or pot and deep-fry until dark golden brown. Do this in 2–3 batches to avoid overcrowding, and skim away any burnt bits with a metal skimmer or strainer in between batches. You can also use an air-fryer or deep-fryer if you have the option.

Serve with lime wedges, mint, cilantro or salad leaves on the side! This is perfect with an ice-cold fizzy drink!

Same same, but different: these meatballs are re-imagined from the Thai salad with herbs, spices and ground toasted rice (also known as *khao kua*).

PORK BELLY STEWED IN COCONUT WATER (THIT KHO TAU)

Coconut water imbues this stew with a very subtle nutty sweetness and, after a couple of hours of hanging out with the fatty meat, it develops and intensifies the pork's latent sweetness. The key here is the initial caramelising of palm sugar, allowing its flavour to deepen before adding the remaining ingredients. You'll want to cook the meat until it is tender and on the verge of falling apart, with the fat just melting when it's on your tongue. Boil some eggs and leave them to steep in the porcine juiciness, then cook up some coconut water-infused rice and you're in business.

SERVES 6–8

1 kg pork belly, cut into 5- to 6-cm chunks (larger pieces will require a longer braising time to become tender)

1 Tbsp canola oil

30 g Thai palm sugar or brown sugar

400 ml water

400 ml coconut water

1¹/₂–2 Tbsp fish sauce, or to taste

2 large red chillies, cut into chunks

Salt to taste

5–7 eggs

MARINADE

4 cloves garlic, peeled

4 shallots, peeled

2 large red chillies

¹/₄ tsp salt

1 tsp fish sauce

Continuing the Feast

Thai palm sugar is used in Wok-Charred Sprouts (p 22), Asian Slaw (p 28), Salmon Belly on a Bed of Herbs (p 48), Thai Steak Salad (p 60) and Rice Porridge with Caramel Pork (p 86).

Coconut water is used in Prawns in Coconut Water and Coconut Water Rice (p 34).

We start by making the marinade for the pork belly. Pound up the garlic, shallots, chillies and salt to form a rough paste. Alternatively, just chop them up together finely. Massage this paste and the fish sauce into the pork belly chunks, then leave to marinate for at least half an hour. I usually do this the night before so it's one less thing to worry about on the day of stewing.

To cook, heat up the oil in a large pot for stewing (a Dutch oven or clay pot would be wonderful here) over medium-low heat. Add the palm sugar and let it caramelise. When its colour has deepen and become almost an amber brown, toss in the pork belly chunks along with its marinade. Sear the pork on all sides, which should take about 2 minutes in total.

Add the water, coconut water, 1¹/₂ tablespoonfuls of fish sauce and chillies. Cover pot partially and let mixture simmer over extremely low heat for 2–3 hours. During this time, occasionally skim away any scum that rises to the surface. The dish is done when the pork belly becomes fall-apart tender.

Boil the eggs for 7 minutes. Arrest the cooking by running tap water over the eggs before peeling them. Place the eggs into the pot and let them stew together with the pork during the final 20–30 minutes of cooking.

Taste the sauce and adjust for seasoning. If it needs more salt, add more fish sauce along with a slight pinch of salt. The taste profile of this is sweet and salty with a back note of spice.

When the meat is done to your liking and the sauce seasoned to perfection, it's time to serve. You can strain the sauce for a clearer finish if you'd like. If not, simply plate and serve with plain rice. I particularly enjoy this with coconut water rice.

Years back, I took my first trip to Vietnam and heard about a dish of chicken stewed in coconut water. I didn't get to try it then, but the idea of a stew made with coconut water never left my mind. When I visited Vietnam recently, I finally managed to taste this traditional Vietnamese dish, stewed with pork belly instead. It was so good that I started to wonder why pork belly was stewed any other way!

STEAMED SPARE RIBS WITH BLACK BEANS

Cantonese cuisine uses a light hand, allowing the flavours of an ingredient to shine through, never overpowering or drowning its essence. Thus, for this classic dim sum dish, keeping things light is essential alongside clean-tasting meat. The fermented black beans used here are pungent and can easily dominate the entire dish if we're not careful. We want to imbue, not attack, the meat with it. Beans, chillies or garlic — no single aromatic should dominate. Instead, they should all work together harmoniously to produce a coveted balance, in food as in life.

SERVES 2

**300 g pork spare ribs, cut into
  2.5- to 4-cm chunks**

**1 ¼ tsp fermented black beans,
  rinsed briefly**

3 tsp light soy sauce

1 tsp white sugar

1 tsp Shaoxing wine

1 tsp sesame oil

1 ½ tsp cornstarch

**Red chillies for garnishing,
  chopped**

**Spring onions for garnishing,
  chopped**

GARLIC OIL

1 Tbsp canola oil

2 cloves garlic, minced

Continuing the Feast
Fermented black beans are used in Beef Noodles with Black Garlic (p 92).

First, prepare the garlic oil. Heat the oil in a small saucepan over low heat and add the garlic. Stir constantly until garlic is lightly golden. Remove from heat, transfer the garlic and oil to a bowl and set aside to cool.

In a heatproof bowl, place the pork ribs with black beans, soy sauce, sugar, Shaoxing wine, sesame oil, cornstarch and garlic oil. Let it marinate for at least an hour or overnight.

To cook, prepare a steaming basket, or a wok with a lid and steaming rack. Bring steaming water to the boil. Over high heat, steam the pork ribs mixture for 10–12 minutes, until tender and infused with flavour.

Garnish with chillies and spring onions, and serve hot.

RICE, NOODZ AND OTHER CARBS

——

> **"***I have made a lot of mistakes falling in love, and regretted most of them, but never the potatoes that went with them.* **"**
>
> **– NORA EPHRON**

BANH MI FORBIDDEN RICE GRAIN BOWL

While banh mi is a traditional Vietnamese dish, we take a detour to Thailand here. Found in Thailand, the black forbidden rice that I'm using isn't the sticky, glutinous sort. It's nutty and hearty, with a purplish hue that makes the grains look like they came from an enchanted forest when plumped up. It's supposed to be packed with antioxidants as well. Feel free to substitute with any other grain you want, like quinoa, red rice or couscous. Here, I'm giving a rough guide to assembling a multi-dimensional grain bowl. There's creamy (good) fat from the avocados, tart crunch from the quick pickles, protein (of course!) in the form of grilled lemongrass-chilli chicken, some verdant green and the scent of summer from a mix of herbs and veggies, and some dry crunchy bits (shallots, peanuts, coconut) scattered on top. If you'd like, you could put an egg on it — a marinated drunken egg (p 51) or a soft-boiled egg.

SERVES 2

200 g forbidden rice (black rice), rinsed

400 ml water

1 portion Grilled Lemongrass-Chilli Chicken (p 57)

Salad leaves, as much as you would like to pile into each bowl

Quick pickles (p 85), as desired

1 avocado, peeled and cubed or sliced

A handful of fresh herbs (basil, mint, cilantro, etc.)

Crispy fried shallots or peanuts for topping

Limes for serving

Sriracha for serving

Continuing the Feast

This grilled chicken is also used in the Bao Mi (p 85).

Leftover salad leaves can be used in Thai Steak Salad (p 60).

Place the rice and water in the rice cooker pot and leave to soak for 1 hour. Cook the rice according to the settings of your rice cooker. When the cooker sings that the rice is done, let the rice hang out inside its sauna for another 15 minutes before opening the lid. If you're using another type of grain, prep and cook according to the package instructions.

As the rice cooks, it's time to grill your lemongrass-chilli chicken. Follow the steps on page 57.

To assemble the rice bowl, scoop a portion of rice into a serving bowl and placing the salad leaves around the rice. Arrange some pickles, the avocado and chicken (sliced or kept whole as you wish) to the side. To garnish, scatter the herbs and crispy fried shallots or peanuts on top.

Serve with cut limes and some sriracha on the side. If you have leftover citrus lemongrass dipping sauce (page 19), you can serve it on the side as an optional dressing.

CRAB FRIED RICE

A waiter placed a lidded earthen bowl in the centre of the table and removed its cover, unveiling a bowl of perfectly fried rice with eggs and lumps of crabmeat, its lemongrass-scented steam wafting visibly upwards. My travel companions and I were starving and this was the first meal we were having upon landing in Vietnam. It was a delight for all our senses that had been previously dulled by the lacklustre plane food.

For *wok hei*, the requisite smoky aroma so prized in a good stir-fry, make sure that your wok is very hot and that you don't overcrowd it. The key is to get everything charred and sizzling before the ingredients become too brittle and dry.

SERVES 1–2

2 Tbsp canola oil or any other neutral-tasting oil

1 stalk lemongrass, bruised

3 cloves garlic, peeled and minced

2 eggs, lightly beaten

240 g cooked rice (leftover is best)

200 g crabmeat (available frozen or canned at supermarkets)

¼ tsp salt

2–3 tsp fish sauce, or to taste

A dash of ground white pepper

1 tsp sesame oil

Crispy fried shallots for garnishing

Any greens of your choice for garnishing (cilantro, spring onion, celery leaves etc.)

Heat a wok over high heat and when it is hot, pour in the canola oil. Turn the heat to low and add the lemongrass, followed by the garlic. Fry until the smallest bits of garlic turn lightly golden.

Tip in the eggs and turn the heat up to high again. Lightly scramble the eggs until they are three-quarters set before adding the rice. Stir-fry over the highest heat possible, mixing the rice and eggs evenly.

Add the crabmeat, salt, fish sauce and pepper. Continue tossing the mixture around the hot wok, until everything takes on a gorgeous, charred note. You'll know the rice is done when it starts popping or dancing inside the wok.

Taste for seasoning and texture. If it isn't salty enough, drizzle in more fish sauce. Switch off the heat, add the sesame oil and mix well. Transfer to serving plates and garnish with some crispy fried shallots and herbs of choice for a pop of freshness.

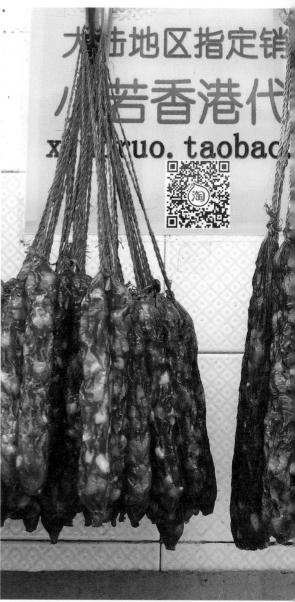

You know that coveted golden brown, crisped parts of rice touching the bottom of the pan, that textural contrast so prized by many cultures all around the world? Yep, all you really need is a very good heavy-bottomed claypot or a Dutch oven to achieve that.

WAXED MEATS RICE (CLAYPOT RICE)

This traditional HK dish is typically eaten during months when the weather is cold and the claypot, piping hot, brings about warmth and energy from its fiery heat and oily cured meats. This recipe was generously shared by the highly skilled and talented Tonny Chan, who runs his namesake Tonny restaurant in Geylang. He cures his own pork belly there, dangling them from the ceiling above his cooking station. He also makes a unique and superb rendition of this using Canadian wild rice wrapped in and perfumed with lotus leaf. Do pre-order this should you wish to it — and you should!

But if you're making this at home instead, all you really need is a very good heavy-bottomed claypot or a Dutch oven. Yep, your trusty Dutch oven will get you that crisp golden brown layer of rice at the bottom of the pan.

SERVES 2-4

300 g jasmine rice

350 ml water

10 g ginger, peeled and cut into thin strips

2 stalks spring onions, white portion only, chopped + more for garnishing

2 Chinese waxed sausage (*lup cheong*), sliced

1 liver Chinese waxed liver sausage (*lup cheong*), sliced

80–100 g cured pork belly, sliced (available at Chinese dried goods shops)

SAUCE

3 Tbsp dark soy sauce

1 Tbsp light soy sauce

2 Tbsp sesame oil or garlic oil or lard

2 Tbsp water

A dash of ground white pepper

Continuing the Feast
Chinese waxed sausage is used in Seared Scallops (p 42) and Radish Cake (p 82).

We start by prepping and soaking our rice. This soaking period allows the rice to cook more evenly. After rinsing and draining your rice well, place it in your cooking vessel of choice — a claypot or Dutch oven — then add the water. Leave to soak for 1–2 hours.

While the rice is soaking, let's prepare our sauce. Simply mix the dark and light soy sauces, oil, water and pepper together. Taste and adjust the seasoning as desired. Set aside.

When you are ready to cook the rice, cover the pot and let it simmer on the lowest possible heat for about 15 minutes, until the water is almost completely absorbed by the rice. Strew the ginger and spring onion slices over — these aromatics will eventually soften in the heat and perfume the rice. Then, arrange the sliced waxed meats and cured pork belly on top, cover the pot and turn the heat to medium. Cook for another 10–15 minutes, allowing the rice at the bottom to crisp up and form a crust. You will hear a sizzling, crackling sound, which means that our rice is getting crisp at the bottom!

Switch off the heat and leave to rest for 5–10 minutes. Serve with the sauce on the side for drizzling over, and garnish with more chopped spring onions if desired.

HK BAKED PORK CHOP RICE

One of the best things that came out of launching my first book was that I got to meet and become friends with more like-minded, food-obsessed people. One of them is Sandra (IG: @Sandrasim), an incredible cook and host who also runs a couple of bars (@SumYiTai). Their retro-chic interiors are all designed by her. This recipe here is contributed by Sandra, and is inspired by one of her favourite dishes in Hong Kong, where she used to live.

If you've never tasted this dish before, I'll break it down for you. The base layer consists of fragrant golden egg fried rice, followed by a couple of juicy marinated pork chops that are smothered with a tomato-ey ketchup sauce. The entire mass is then bound together by stringy, gooey cheese. It's the sort of dish that would please kids and inner-kids alike.

SERVES 4

500 g pork chops, about 4 chops

4 Tbsp canola oil or any other neutral-tasting oil

160 g grated mozzarella cheese

MARINADE

2 cloves garlic, peeled and minced

1 tsp minced ginger

A dash of ground white pepper

2 tsp cornstarch

1 tsp white sugar

1 Tbsp oyster sauce

1 Tbsp Shaoxing wine

1 Tbsp sesame oil

1 Tbsp Maggi seasoning

EGG FRIED RICE

350 g cooked rice, left overnight

3 eggs

1/2 tsp salt

1 tsp sesame oil

1 tsp chicken powder

Ground white pepper to taste

2 Tbsp canola oil

Light soy sauce to taste

TOMATO SAUCE

8–10 Tbsp ketchup, or to taste

1 tsp Maggi seasoning

1 tsp light soy sauce

2 Tbsp white sugar

1 tsp chicken powder

A dash of white pepper

1 yellow onion, peeled, halved and each half cut into 3–4 chunks lengthwise

3 tomatoes, cut into chunks

We start by tenderising and marinating the pork chops. Using the back of a knife, a rolling pin or a meat mallet, you wanna pound the chops until they're slightly flattened. Combine all the marinade ingredients and pour it over the chops. Leave to marinate for a couple of hours or, ideally, overnight.

For the egg fried rice, place the rice in a large mixing bowl and add eggs, salt, sesame oil, chicken powder and pepper. Mix until well combined.

Heat a wok or large saucepan over high heat and add the cooking oil. When the oil is hot, add the rice mixture and stir-fry until lightly golden brown and charred. Add soy sauce according to taste. Transfer to an ovenproof baking pan — a casserole or cast-iron pan would work as well. We'll get back to this in a bit.

To a large sauté pan, add 4 tablespoonfuls of oil and heat over medium-high heat until the oil is hot. Using a pair of tongs, place your chops in the pan. Sear on both sides until nicely golden. You don't have to worry about them being fully cooked at this point, since they'll be finished off in the oven. Arrange the seared chops on top of the egg fried rice.

To make the tomato sauce, mix the ketchup, Maggi seasoning, soy sauce, sugar, chicken powder and pepper together in a bowl. In the same pan used for searing the chops, heat onion chunks over high heat. Stir them around before adding the tomatoes and cooking for about 45 seconds.

Add ketchup mixture and about 150 ml water. Let the mixture come to a boil and reduce until it thickens, about a couple of minutes. Taste and adjust for seasoning. If you want a stronger tomato flavour, add an extra 1–2 tablespoonfuls of ketchup. If you want a thinner sauce, splash in more water a little at a time, until the desired consistency is achieved.

Continuing the Feast

Tomatoes and ketchup are used in Tomato Egg (p 58).

Chicken powder is used in Radish Cake (p 82) and Vietnamese Chicken Porridge (p 88).

Smother the chops with the tomato sauce and top generously with mozzarella cheese. You can make this ahead of time and leave it in the refrigerator overnight or a few hours until you're ready to serve.

To serve, preheat the oven to 175°C. Bake for 8–10 minutes, until the cheese gets all bubbly, golden and burnished.

Serve and dig into your bowl of gooey, cheesy carbs.

JACKFRUIT KRA POW

I might actually prefer this to the typical kra pow with meat because it is incredibly smoky, sweet and spicy, and an absolute delight to wolf down. If you haven't tried jackfruit in savoury dishes in lieu of meat, you really have to. Unlike many other fruits, jackfruit doesn't become mushy when exposed to heat. Instead, it takes on a lovely, yielding and almost meaty texture, and its sweetness is amplified. If you want to keep things vegan, omit the egg and replace the fish sauce with more light soy sauce instead. If you're cooking this for a larger group of people, I'd suggest making this in small batches anyway so that your wok stays hot and smoky. If you can't get your hands on Thai holy basil, feel free to use sweet basil instead.

SERVES 1

1 bird's eye chilli

1 clove garlic, peeled

1 shallot, peeled

3¹/₂ Tbsp canola oil

120 g jackfruit, cut into 0.5-cm cubes

¹/₂ tsp light soy sauce

1 tsp dark soy sauce

¹/₂ tsp fish sauce

A bunch of Thai holy basil or sweet basil leaves

1 egg

Continuing the Feast
Jackfruit is used in Smoky Chicken Soup (p 114).

Begin by cooking some Thai jasmine rice. The ratio for this is 1 cup rice to 1¹/₄ cups water. For convenience, I use a rice cooker and the setting for white rice.

While the rice is cooking, work on the aromatics. If using a mortar and pestle, pound the chilli, garlic and shallot together to form a paste. Alternatively, use a knife to individually mince them and combine.

Heat a wok over medium-low heat and add 1¹/₂ tablespoonfuls of oil. When the oil is hot, add the paste and stir-fry until it is lightly browned. Add the jackfruit cubes and turn the heat to high. Give everything a good stir and let the jackfruit and paste char together.

Drizzle in the light and dark soy sauces and fish sauce. Toss to combine and continue to cook until the mixture begins to caramelise. Add a small splash of water, about 2 tablespoonfuls, and continue stirring.

Toss in the basil leaves. Stir until they wilt and switch off the heat immediately.

For the fried egg topping, heat a clean wok over high heat and add 2 tablespoonfuls of oil. When the oil is hot, add the egg and allow its edges to crisp up. Cover your wok to allow the top of the egg to set. Check to make sure the yolk is cooked to your desired doneness, then switch off the heat and set the egg aside.

To serve, plate a mound of steamed jasmine rice — or use whatever carb you desire or have on hand — then arrange the jackfruit stir-fry on top. Plop the egg on the side and you're done!

RADISH CAKE (LOR BAK GO)

While I was in Hong Kong, I had the great pleasure of taking a peek at the workings of a Cantonese restaurant, courtesy of Lai Shi Fu, the chef in charge of its dim sum station. He's been in this trade since he was a young boy, and has learned the ropes and slowly climbed the kitchen hierarchy. Despite being trained the old-school way, he also embraces creativity in cuisine, stating that as in life, everything evolves and we've got to keep up. Perhaps it's a kind of savvy that is required when you're living in a city like Hong Kong, where you've got to be adaptable and quick.

This traditional dim sum recipe was given to me by Lai Shi Fu with the hopes of preserving some aspects of his dwindling lifelong trade. It's so old school that the quantities of ingredients are measured in "catties" and "taels". His daughter, Joanne, has kindly translated these measurements for us. I've scaled down the recipe a little and added some dried scallops and mushrooms to luxe things up a bit. Otherwise, it's the recipe as stated by Lai Shi Fu. You could also mix things up and replace the *lup cheong* with some smoky bacon or Spanish ham.

MAKES ONE 23-CM ROUND CAKE

3 dried Chinese mushrooms

1 Chinese waxed sausage (*lup cheong*), about 60 g, skin removed, meat chopped into tiny chunks

60 g dried shrimps

20 g dried scallops

700 g Chinese white radish, coarsely grated or julienned

Sesame oil for greasing

500 ml soaking liquid (see method)

150 g rice flour

10 g cornstarch

10 g potato starch

1 Tbsp MSG

1 Tbsp light soy sauce

1 tsp chicken powder

35 g white sugar

1 tsp ground white pepper

1¼ tsp salt, or to taste

3 Tbsp canola oil

Continuing the Feast

Chinese waxed sausage is used in Seared Scallops (p 42) and Waxed Meats Rice (p 77).

Dried scallops are used in Somen with Clams (p 107), Superior Stock (p 124) and Premium Udon Soup (p 134).

Chinese white radish is used in Vegetarian Pho (p 118) and Vegan Tom Yum (p 130).

Chicken powder is used in Baked Pork Chop Rice (p 78) and Vietnamese Chicken Porridge (p 88).

MSG is used in Vegan Tom Yum (p 130).

First, prep the dried ingredients. Soak the dried mushrooms in water for a couple of hours until they soften. Reserve the soaking liquid, dice mushrooms into tiny cubes and set aside with the sausage. Soak dried shrimps and scallops in water for 10 minutes. Reserve the soaking liquid and chop both shrimps and scallops into little chunks. Set aside.

Sprinkle about ½ teaspoonful of salt over the grated radish and leave to sit for about 10 minutes. This will draw out liquid, which we will put to good use later on.

Grease a 23-cm (9-in) round cake pan or a 20-cm (8-in) square aluminium pan with sesame oil. Get into each nook and cranny, then line the bottom of the pan with parchment paper.

Drain the radish and reserve extracted liquid to combine with all the soaking liquid set aside earlier. In a large bowl, add 500 ml of this mixture, along with rice flour, cornstarch, potato starch, MSG, soy sauce, chicken powder, sugar, pepper and salt. Whisk to mix well, taste the batter and adjust seasoning as desired.

Heat canola oil in a large Dutch oven or wok over medium heat. When the oil is hot, add the mushrooms and sausage, frying them until they start to brown slightly. Tip in the scallops and shrimps. After 10–12 minutes, when the mixture is toasty and fragrant, add the grated radish. If you prefer, you could also fry the dried ingredients individually, then combine them at the end. Let the radish cook for about 5 minutes, until it softens and soaks up all the flavourful juices.

Turn the heat to low and trickle in the batter, making sure to stir constantly and scrape the bottom of the pot. Keep stirring and scraping for 5–7 minutes, as you allow the batter to thicken into the consistency of heavy wet sludge.

Transfer the batter into the prepare pan and smooth over the top before steaming over high heat for 40–45 minutes. Leave to cool to room temperature, then place in the refrigerator to firm up for at least a couple of hours but preferably overnight.

To pan-fry into dim sum-style cakes, cut the cooked cake into squares or rectangles. Heat a pan with some oil over medium heat. When the pan is hot, place the cakes in and sear on all sides until they turn crusty and golden. Serve with chilli sauce or sliced chillies in some light soy sauce.

BAO MI

In pizza, it's the bread dough that make-th the dish, and likewise in the case of banh mi, it's the Vietnamese bread that does so. No matter how mind-blowing the fillings or toppings are, if the bread isn't spectacular too, the entire experience is diminished. The Vietnamese baguette is a whole other (lighter) specimen. Its gossamer-thin crust crackles into brittle shards and gives way to an airy, super fluffy interior that's all too easy to wolf down. The kind made from rice flour and magic. It's hard to procure this level of goodness outside of Vietnam, so I've substituted them with Chinese bao buns that are slightly sweet and will fluff up when steamed. Bonus: Any leftovers can be refurbished, with a couple extra additions, into another meal a la Forbidden Rice Grain Bowl.

SERVES 6

1 portion Grilled Lemongrass-Chilli Chicken (p 57)

6 Chinese bao buns

Cilantro leaves for garnishing

Crispy fried shallots for garnishing

QUICK PICKLES

45 g mix of carrot and radish, julienned

2 Tbsp white vinegar

2 tsp white sugar

A pinch of salt

SIRACHA MAYO

60 g Japanese mayonnaise

35 g sriracha

Continuing the Feast
The quick pickles are used in Forbidden Rice Grain Bowl (p 72).

We start by preparing the quick pickles. Place the carrot and radish mix, vinegar, sugar and salt in a bowl. Leave to hang out together for about 20 minutes, before draining the vegetables and lightly squeezing them dry.

Prepare the lemongrass-chilli chicken according to the steps on page 57. Leave the chicken to rest before cutting into chunks or slices.

For the sriracha mayo, mix the mayonnaise and sriracha together.

To assemble your bao mi, steam your bao buns over high heat until they are heated through and softened, about 5 minutes. Remove from heat and leave to cool slightly.

Pry open each bun with the back of a spoon, before smearing the sriracha mayo on the insides. Place a few chunks of chicken on one side, then top with pickles, cilantro leaves and crispy fried shallots. Repeat to use up the rest of the chicken chunks.

Serve while buns are still piping hot.

RICE PORRIDGE WITH CARAMEL PORK AND BLACK GARLIC

Years ago, I saw an Asian American contestant, Mei Lin, win a challenge on *Top Chef* season 12 with this dish. It received such rave reviews from the judges and made me so curious about the flavour combination that I just had to make it. Back then, I didn't have access to black garlic but the flavours were already mind-blowing. The familiar blandness of plain congee is the perfect foil for letting the caramelised pork shine. Coconut palm sugar lends a butterscotch sweetness, light soy gives a salty dimension, and the black garlic contributes a pruney and almost wine-like complexity. A small splash of black vinegar brings an elevated finish. Be daring with the white pepper here as the dish can, and should, withstand some warmth.

SERVES 2

100 g Japanese short grain rice, rinsed

1.2 litres water

Cilantro leaves for garnishing

Crispy fried shallots for garnishing (see method)

CARAMEL PORK

1 Tbsp canola oil

300 g minced pork

2 Tbsp light soy sauce, or more to taste

30 g Thai palm sugar

1 head black garlic, peeled, mashed and mixed with 1 Tbsp water

¼ cup water

2 tsp black vinegar

A large dash of white pepper

Spring onions for garnishing, chopped

Continuing the Feast

Black garlic is used in Beef Noodles with Black Garlic (p 92).

Japanese short grain rice is used in Vietnamese Chicken Porridge (p 88).

Thai palm sugar is used in Wok-Charred Sprouts (p 22), Asian Slaw (p 28), Salmon Belly on a Bed of Herbs (p 48), Thai Steak Salad (p 60) and Pork Belly Stew (p 66).

For the porridge, place your rice and 1.2 litres water in a pot and bring to the boil. Cook over medium-low heat until the grains are soft and swollen, which should take 20–25 minutes.

While the rice is cooking, make the caramel pork topping. Heat the oil in a saucepan over medium-high heat. When the oil is hot, add the minced pork and break it up using a spatula. Spread out the meat and let it brown — after the juices are released and evaporated, keep stirring the pork to brown it evenly. Add 1 tablespoonful of soy sauce to season, then set aside.

In the same saucepan used to cook the minced pork, melt palm sugar over low heat and let it caramelise briefly. This should take about 30 seconds. Stir in 1 tablespoonful of soy sauce and the black garlic paste, letting the flavours cook and meld together.

Add the pork back into the pan with all of its remaining juices, as well as the water. Stir and adjust the heat to medium. Let the mixture reduce until the sauce clings onto the pork and the mixture is darkened and caramelised.

Remove from heat before adding the black vinegar and pepper. Taste and adjust seasoning as desired, then top with chopped spring onions.

To serve, dish out porridge into individual bowls. Spoon the caramel pork over and top with cilantro leaves, more spring onions, and crispy fried shallots if using.

To make crispy fried shallots, peel and thinly slice as many shallots as desired. In a wok or saucepan over medium-low heat, add enough oil so that it would just cover the shallots. When the oil is hot, add the shallots and turn the heat to low to prevent burning. Fry until lightly golden before removing the shallots from the oil and draining them on paper towels. They will continue to cook and darken as they cool, so don't wait until they are golden brown to take them out.

Be daring with the white pepper here as this dish can, and should, withstand some warmth.

VIETNAMESE CHICKEN PORRIDGE

The night air was cool and breezy, the traffic hectic and blaring as the neon lights were twinkling in preparation for Tet, the Vietnamese New Year. My friends and I strolled pass the roadside stalls selling pre-packed snacks, people peddling their toys, and couples in love lounging on their motorbikes. Suddenly, there we were at our next destination, which Cuong (the man who founded Red Boat) had picked for us: a place that specialised in chicken dishes. Chicken pho, chicken porridge, chicken steamed and piled on top of sticky rice, and also chicken salad. On that balmy night, I was feeling slightly under the weather, and this bowl of chicken porridge was just about the best thing I tasted. It was a simple porridge done exceedingly well, full of pure chicken-y flavour. It came with a bunch of chopped up herbs — not mere garnish, but a large sprinkle of greens swirling through the rice grains.

And boy, was it chicken porridge for the soul. You know what tastes more like chicken than chicken itself? The essence of chicken captured intensely in chicken powder. To replicate that chicken-y taste, I throw in a couple spoonfuls of that, but it's completely optional.

SERVES 2-3

150 g Japanese short grain rice

10 g kombu

1 stalk spring onion, white portion only + a bunch of spring onions for garnishing, sliced

1.2 litres water or chicken stock

2 whole chicken legs, skin and bone intact

3½ tsp chicken powder (the saltiness depends on the brand you use, so taste and adjust)

Salt or fish sauce, to taste

Tons of cilantro, chopped

Continuing the Feast

Japanese short grain rice is used in Rice Porridge with Caramel Pork (p 86).

Kombu is used in Fish Congee (p 91), Somen with Clams (p 107), Sesame Chicken Somen (p 117), Superior Stock (p 124) and Vegan Tom Yum (p 130).

Chicken powder is used in Baked Pork Chop Rice (p 78) and Radish Cake (p 82).

Prep your rice by washing it and draining well. Gently wipe the kombu with a damp cloth.

Place the rice, kombu, 1 stalk spring onion, water and chicken legs in a large stockpot. Let everything simmer over the lowest possible heat for 1.5 hours, stirring it once in awhile, especially towards the end, to make sure that nothing gets stuck at the bottom of the pot.

Switch off the heat, then remove the chicken legs to let cool on the side. Remove the kombu and give the porridge a stir. The consistency should be slightly starchy and rice grains should still be visibly intact. Season to taste with the chicken powder and salt. Leave to stand for 15–20 minutes to thicken and let flavours develop.

Shred the meat from the chicken legs and return the meat to the pot. Reheat the porridge until it's piping hot and portion into bowls. Top with a bunch of cilantro and sliced spring onions.

Serve with ground white pepper as desired and prepare to experience this porridge's soul-warming effects.

The grains are semi disintegrated but still visible, while their texture slightly thick but not overly so. It's somewhere between congee and rice porridge. I find that good quality Japanese rice has just that perfect amount of starch that helps the porridge get this texture.

The key to all that flavour is pork leg bones, which happen to be cheap and available at a butcher's. They lend that sweet, milky taste that will push your congee from great to sublime.

FISH CONGEE WITH SHREDDED GINGER

The first meal I had when I touched down in Hong Kong was a piping hot bowl of comforting, velvety smooth and creamy congee at Ho Hung Kee. It came with pristine white fish slices and tons of ginger shards. And the congee tasted like nothing I've ever had before. The key to all that flavour is pork leg bones, which happen to be cheap and available at a butcher's. They lend that sweet, milky taste that will push your congee from great to sublime.

You could make a stock with the bones first, then use the stock to cook your congee for another few hours. But if you're like me and prefer a more efficient (read: lazy) method, just cook the congee with plain water and add the pork leg bones. People will think you slaved all day over the stove, but really, there's nothing much to do after it's all in the pot, just a little vigilance here and there while you get on with other tasks on hand. Trust me, you *can* have restaurant-quality congee in your own home with minimal fuss.

SERVES 4

400 g pork leg bones

100 g jasmine rice

50 g glutinous rice

1 slice ginger

1 stalk spring onion, white portion only

4-cm square of kombu

2 tsp salt, or to taste

2 litres water

80 ml unsweetened soy milk

SLICED FISH

450 g grouper fillet, cut into chunks

1 tsp fine sea salt

A dash of ground white pepper

3 tsp Shaoxing wine

1 tsp sesame oil

GARNISHING

Spring onions, sliced

Young ginger, peeled and finely shredded

Continuing the Feast

Kombu is used in Vietnamese Chicken Porridge (p 88), Somen with Clams (p 107), Sesame Chicken Somen (p 117), Superior Stock (p 124) and Vegan Tom Yum (p 130).

Glutinous rice is used in Laab Meatballs (p 64).

We start by blanching the pork leg bones. To do this, place the bones in a saucepan of water and bring to a rolling boil. Allow it to boil for 15 minutes. This gets rid of impurities and scum, which is crucial, as we will not be making a stock that can be strained before use.

While the pork leg bones are being blanched, place the jasmine rice, glutinous rice, ginger, spring onion, kombu, salt and water in a large stockpot.

Drain the pork bones and rinse them well. Add the bones to the stockpot and bring everything to a simmer over the lowest possible heat — this will keep the scum to a minimum. Use a spoon to skim away any more scum that rises. Let simmer for about 3 hours, occasionally stirring to ensure nothing sticks to the bottom of the pot.

While the rice is cooking, marinate the fish with salt, pepper, Shaoxing wine and sesame oil. Cover with cling film and refrigerate until needed.

After 3 hours, use a pair of tongs to remove the pork bones, ginger and spring onion. Let the congee continue to cook and reduce, stirring frequently. This will take another 15–30 minutes, depending on how thick you prefer the congee to be.

When the consistency is to your liking, add the soy milk and adjust the seasoning to taste.

Add the marinated fish chunks and cook until they just turn opaque. Portion into individual bowls and serve garnished with spring onions and ginger.

BEEF NOODLES WITH BLACK GARLIC AND BLACK BEAN GRAVY

Black garlic partners with funky, salty fermented black beans like a dream. Their earthy notes complement each other and the garlic adds another dimension to this traditional Cantonese stir-fry — a little sweet, sticky and slightly tart action to awaken your palate. Here, the noodles are first charred to add some smoky depth before being introduced to the flavour-laden garlicky black sauce. Then, to gild the lily, garnish with some fried garlic bits to echo all the garlicky notes within.

SERVES 2–3

150 g flank, skirt or rib-eye steak, thinly sliced, or beef stir-fry strips

25 g black garlic, about 1 head, skin removed

1 clove garlic, peeled and minced

1 large red chilli, minced

1 tsp fermented black beans, rinsed and lightly crushed

600 ml chicken stock or vegetable stock, unsalted

1 Tbsp light soy sauce

1 tsp dark soy sauce

1/2 tsp fish sauce

1/2 tsp salt

1/2 tsp freshly cracked black pepper

1 tsp sesame oil

400 g fresh flat rice noodles (*hor fun*)

A bunch of leafy greens like Chinese broccoli (*gai lan*) or bok choy

4 1/2 Tbsp cornstarch mixed with 4 Tbsp water to form a slurry

A splash of Shaoxing wine

MARINADE

2 1/2 tsp light soy sauce

1 tsp sesame oil

2 tsp Shaoxing wine

1 tsp potato starch

1/2 tsp ground black pepper

1/2 tsp white sugar

CRISPY FRIED GARLIC

4–5 cloves garlic, peeled

Enough canola oil to cover garlic

Continuing the Feast
Black garlic is used in Rice Porridge with Caramel Pork (p 86).

Fermented black beans are used in Spare Ribs with Black Beans (p 68).

Combine all the marinade ingredients and beef strips in a bowl. Leave to marinate as you prepare the crispy fried garlic.

You can prepare the fried garlic from scratch or use store-bought fried garlic chips if it's more convenient. If prepping your own, simply mince the garlic and add to a saucepan. Pour 60–80 ml oil to just cover the garlic, then heat over low heat and fry until lightly golden brown. There's a fine line between toasty golden and burnt garlic here. Immediately transfer the garlic into a bowl to prevent it from darkening any further and set aside. Reserve the garlic oil as we'll be using it to cook the rest of the dish.

Prep the garlic and bean paste. Mash the black garlic using the back of a spoon until it becomes a paste. Combine with the minced garlic, chilli and fermented black beans. Set aside.

In a bowl or jug, mix the stock with light and dark soy sauces, fish sauce, salt, black pepper and sesame oil. Set aside.

To char the noodles, heat a wok over high heat and add the 2 tablespoonfuls of reserved garlic oil. When the oil is hot, add the flat rice noodles and stir-fry for 40–50 seconds, until the edges are charred and crisp. Transfer noodles to a plate and set aside.

In the same wok, heat up 1 tablespoonful of garlic oil over high heat. Add the beef slices and allow them to sear. When they are nearly cooked, add the vegetables and give them a quick toss through. Transfer the beef and vegetables to a plate and set aside.

We'll now get on with the black garlic and black bean gravy. Add 1 1/2 tablespoonfuls of garlic oil to the wok and reduce the heat to medium-low. Add the garlic and bean paste and fry lightly until its fragrance is released, about 40 seconds or so. Pour in the seasoned stock and let everything come to a boil. Reduce the heat to low and add three-quarters of the cornstarch slurry. Check that the consistency is to your liking. If a thicker gravy is desired, add the remaining slurry. Splash in the Shaoxing wine.

Add the beef, vegetables and noodles to the wok and cook until everything is heated up and well mixed. Taste and adjust seasoning as desired. Pile noodles onto a serving plate and scatter crispy fried garlic on top.

TURMERIC BEEF NOODLES WITH PINEAPPLE MINT SALSA

These noodles are stained a pleasing yellow with sunset-hued turmeric, which has a spicy warmth to jolt you awake. A super flavourful marinade penetrates the beef slices, seasoning and tenderising the meat inside out. Finally, a lovely, well-chilled pineapple and mint salsa is served alongside the noodles as a cooling contrast. Although this looks and feels like such a feast, it's so straightforward to put together, I file it under the category of "dishes for weeknight meals". By the way, this is the perfect place to start stir-frying noodles if you're new to it — these thick rice vermicelli noodles are one of the easiest to work with in a wok.

SERVES 2–3

150 g beef stir-fry slices (you can get away with cheaper cuts here)

45 g chives, washed and pat dry

2–3 Tbsp canola oil or any other neutral-tasting oil

300 g fresh rice vermicelli

1– 2 tsp fish sauce

Salt, to taste

MARINADE

2 stalks lemongrass

1 large red chilli

2 shallots, peeled

2 cloves garlic, peeled

30 g turmeric, peeled

1 1/4 tsp oyster sauce

3/4 tsp fish sauce

A pinch of salt

3/4 tsp white sugar

1 tsp sesame oil

Ground black pepper to taste

PINEAPPLE MINT SALSA

80 g pineapple, peeled and cubed

1 tsp fish sauce

2 tsp white sugar, or to taste

A bunch of fresh mint, torn

A squeeze of lime juice

First, let's get on with the marinade that will work its magic on the beef slices and eventually flavour your noodles. For the lemongrass, remove the tough outer leaves and use only the tender inner stems of the bottom half. Cut the chilli into large chunks, then roughly chop the shallots and garlic.

If using a mortar and pestle, start by pounding the turmeric into a rough paste. Add the lemongrass and pound well, following it with the garlic, shallots and chilli. This will yield a rough orange-hued paste. Alternatively, blitz everything up in a food processor, or use a knife and chopping board to get everything minced before mixing them together.

Put the beef slices in a bowl and add the paste, oyster sauce, fish sauce, salt, sugar, sesame oil and pepper. Mix well and let the beef absorb all that wonderful flavour for 20–30 minutes.

In the meantime, prepare the pineapple mint salsa. Mix the pineapple cubes with the fish sauce, sugar and mint. Squeeze some lime juice over and mix well. Taste and adjust to your liking. Leave in the refrigerator to chill as you pull everything together in the wok.

Chop and discard the top and bottom 2-cm ends of the chives before cutting the remaining portion into 5- to 6-cm lengths.

Heat a wok over medium-high heat. When the wok is hot, swirl in the oil. Add the beef and all of its marinade. Scrape the bowl clean — you don't want to miss out a single drop. Give everything a good swirl and sear, about 30 seconds.

Add the rice vermicelli and toss everything around to cook evenly. Season with 1 teaspoonful of fish sauce and a small pinch of salt. Continue tossing everything as you add the chives. Let them wilt for 10–15 seconds before switching off the heat. The entire cooking process will not take more than 5 minutes.

Taste the noodles to see if it's seasoned to your liking. If not, drizzle in a little more fish sauce and toss well. Serve the chilled pineapple-mint salsa to go with it.

BACON PAD SEE EW

Frankly, this dish came about when I was making a noodle stir-fry for a quick lunch and couldn't be bothered to procure a whole hunk of protein, use only a sliver and then freeze up the rest (freezer real estate is prime in this household). But what do I *always* have on hand in my freezer? Rashes of streaky bacon. So they sub in for the protein here and their fat is rendered to flavour the noodles — you don't have to use lard for this; you get it *instantly*. A win-win! *Pad see ew* isn't meant to be a saucy stir-fry; it's more of a dry fry and char. But if things start to look a little too dry, just add in a tiny splash of water to move things along. Also, I wouldn't recommend stir-frying a huge batch of these noodles. Small batches give you the requisite smokiness and charred surface you desire in wok-fried noodles. And I mean, bacon, eggs, carbs!

SERVES 1–2

1 Tbsp canola oil

3 rashes bacon, cut into thin slices

2 cloves garlic, peeled and minced

2 eggs

300 g fresh flat rice noodles

50 g baby Chinese broccoli
  (*gai lan*) or bok choy (or any
  other leafy green you prefer)

1 tsp light soy sauce

1 tsp dark soy sauce

1 1/4 tsp fish sauce, or to taste

Ground white pepper to taste

PICKLED CHILLIES (OPTIONAL)

Large red chillies

Rice vinegar to cover the chillies

Continuing the Feast
Fresh flat rice noodles are used in Beef Noodles with Black Garlic (p 92).

Heat a wok over high heat, and when it is hot, add the oil. Turn the heat to medium-low and toss in your bacon slices. Stir-fry the bacon, allowing it to lightly crisp up and its fat to render.

When the bacon is almost browned, add the garlic and stir quickly until the mixture is fragrant. Add the eggs and leave for 10–15 seconds to set lightly before continuing to stir-fry. Push the eggs, bacon and garlic to one side of the wok, then add the rice noodles on the empty side.

Using the back of the spatula, press the rice noodles against the hot, searing wok. This will help develop a better char. Throw in the vegetables and toss everything around, alternating between stir-frying and pressing the noodles against the wok for charring.

At this point, add the light and dark soy sauces, fish sauce and pepper. Continue to stir-fry until a nice charred exterior develops and you're happy with what you see. Taste and adjust for seasoning before transferring to a serving plate.

Serve with pickled chillies if desired.

For the pickled chillies, just slice the chillies and submerge them in rice vinegar. Let them hang out for at least 15 minutes and ta-da, you've got yourself some quick pickled chillies to serve alongside your noodle stir-fry.

CHILLI BEEF NOODZ

The beauty of a long and slow braise is that it transforms, without much effort on your part, a watery mixture into a velvety sauce coating chunks of meat and ready to be draped over all manner of carbs like wheat noodles, pasta or potatoes. There are few things in life that are as assured as marinating and stewing a (cheapish) cut of meat until it succumbs to yielding tenderness. The margin of error is much smaller here (close to zero) compared to that of searing a steak until medium-rare. Those are good odds for any home cook. Here, chunks of beef are braised in spice mixture that features *doubanjeang*, which amps up the flavour like you would not believe. After a few hours of stewing, plop the braised beef on top of starchy and chewy *la mian* and served with a light scatter of spring onions.

SERVES 4–6

800 g beef shin (or brisket, cheek, ribs, or any cut suited for slow-braising)

2–3 Tbsp canola oil

15 g ginger, peeled and smashed

4 cloves garlic, peeled and smashed

½ red onion or a few shallots, peeled and sliced

4 stalks spring onions, green and white portions separated, both portions chopped

2–3 dried chillies

1 stick cinnamon

1 star anise

2 Tbsp dark soy sauce

2 Tbsp light soy sauce

2½ Tbsp *doubanjeang* (chilli bean paste)

1.5–2 litres water

½ tsp white sugar

Salt to taste

4–6 servings of fresh *la mian* noodles or dried noodles of choice

Continuing the Feast
Cinnamon sticks and star anise are used in Tea-Smoked Duck Legs (p 52), Braised Beef Brisket (p 63) and Vegetarian Pho (p 118).

First, cut your hunk of beef into 5-cm (2-in) chunks and set aside.

In a Dutch oven or your stewing vessel of choice, heat the oil over medium-low heat. When the oil is hot, add the aromatics — ginger, garlic, red onion and the white portion of the spring onions. Let these soften for a bit before adding the dried chillies, cinnamon and star anise. When the mixture is fragrant, crank the heat up to high and add the beef chunks to sear on all sides.

Mix in the dark and light soy sauces and *doubanjeang*, then let it all cook together for a bit. Add enough water to cover the meat, then clamp the lid on. Reduce the heat to low and bring the mixture to a simmer. Let this stew for 3–4 hours until the beef is tender, checking and stirring occasionally. If you feel that the liquid is evaporating a little too quickly, just top up with more water.

When the beef is tender, remove the lid and let the stew reduce until the desired consistency. Here's the time to adjust the seasoning with sugar and salt. As you'll be serving these over noodles, you can afford it tasting a bit more savoury.

To serve, cook your noodles of choice. Drain and coat with a drizzle of sesame oil to prevent clumping. Plop into serving bowls, then ladle over the braised chilli beef. Don't forget the delicious velvety sauce! Sprinkle the chopped green portion of spring onions on top and serve.

XO SCALLOP NOODLES with CHEESE

This dish came about when I was rummaging through the fridge and pantry for something quick to put together. A couple rounds of dried egg noodles, (I used thin, shrimp-flavoured ones from Hong Kong, but even instant noodles would do) dollops of store-bought XO sauce and a couple of seared scallops later, et voilà! I gild the lily by adding a blanket of cheese to pull everything together and to act as a foil to all the spice. As for the cheese, you can use any type of cheese that melts well. If you have a blowtorch, it's time to whip it out. If not, a quick blast under a hot oven or just stirring the cheese through the hot noodles in the wok would all work.

SERVES 2

135 g dried egg noodles

6 scallops

Salt to taste

Ground black pepper to taste

3–4 Tbsp canola oil

3 eggs, beaten

4–5 Tbsp XO sauce

1 tsp light soy sauce, or to taste

3–4 Tbsp water or stock

100 g grated mozzarella cheese or a few slices of processed cheese

Continuing the Feast
XO sauce is used in French Beans Amandine (p 27), Porridge Kueh Stir-Fry (p 102).

Cook the noodles according to the package instructions. They can be slightly undercooked by about 30 seconds as they'll be cooked further later. Drain and toss with some sesame oil to prevent them from sticking together.

Using paper towels, pat the scallops as dry as possible. This will help them achieve golden deliciousness when searing. Season both sides of the scallops with salt and pepper.

Heat a wok or saucepan over high heat and add 2–3 tablespoonfuls of oil. When the oil is hot, use a pair of tongs to place the scallops in the pan. Leave them for a minute or so to sear until a crust develops. Do not flip or disturb them. When the golden crust is a little visible from the sides, flip the scallops and allow the other side to cook and char, about another 40 seconds. Set aside.

Heat a wok over high heat and then drizzle in about 2 tablespoonfuls of oil. Add in the eggs and leave to cook like an omelette until about 70 per cent done. Break up the eggs with a good stir and then toss in your noodles. Stir-fry and let the noodles char.

Season with the XO sauce and soy sauce, stirring to mix thoroughly. Loosen the mixture by adding the water. Continue stir-frying everything until the noodles are fragrant and lightly charred. Taste and adjust seasoning.

At this point, you can choose to do one of two things. You could mix in your cheese to let it melt into delicious gooeyness in the heat of the wok. Otherwise, you could plop your noodles onto a plate, top with the cheese and torch with a blowtorch until golden brown. You could also give it a quick blast it in the oven preheated to 200°C until the cheese is melted, about 5 minutes. Arrange the scallops on top right before serving.

PORRIDGE KUEH STIR-FRY WITH XO SAUCE AND PRAWNS

Porridge kueh is a traditional Hokkien "noodle" that's made from leftover porridge and tapioca starch. You're basically making your own noodle dough but without using a rolling pin or pasta machine, and this results in a chewy, springy textured noodle that works superbly in stir-fries. I shared the way my great-grandma and grandma would make this dish in my first book. I saw Geraldine (@Thatgreedypig on IG) put a spin on that by stir-frying the porridge kueh with prawns, egg and XO sauce. Inspired, I did my own take on it and added a beautifully mottled century egg.

SERVES 2

2 Tbsp canola oil or lard

5–6 prawns, shells removed

2 cloves garlic, peeled and minced

1 shallot, peeled and minced

1 bird's eye chilli, minced

2–3 Tbsp XO sauce

1–2 Tbsp water

2 tsp light soy sauce, or to taste

1/2 tsp dark soy sauce

A pinch of salt, or to taste

A pinch of ground white pepper, or to taste

2 eggs, cracked into a bowl

60 g bean sprouts

1 century egg (optional), peeled and cut into chunks (optional)

Cilantro for garnishing

DOUGH

150 g cooked rice porridge (make sure it's as thick as possible and not at all watery)

160–200 g tapioca starch

> **Continuing the Feast**
> *XO sauce is used in French Beans Amandine (p 27) and XO Scallop Noodles (p 101).*
>
> *Century egg is used in Trio-Egg Spinach (p 128).*

To prepare the dough, combine the porridge and tapioca starch in a bowl, and knead until a smooth dough forms. The amount of flour needed will depend on how watery the porridge is. Start with a little tapioca starch and add more as you go along. The end product should be slightly tacky but easy to work with.

Start a pot of water boiling. When the dough is smooth, pinch rounds of it and form into flat sheets. Drop the dough sheets into the boiling water to cook in batches. They are done when they turn opaque white and float. Drain and set aside.

Place the dough sheets in a single layer on a tray or plate. Cover with cling film, and repeat by laying another layer of dough sheets on top and wrapping with cling film. Do this until all dough sheets are covered. The cling film layers prevent the dough sheets from sticking to each other. Refrigerate for a couple of hours, or preferably overnight, until chilled and firm. Before beginning to stir-fry, cut dough sheets into rectangular strips.

For the stir-fry, heat a wok over high heat. When the wok is hot, add the oil and heat until smoky. Toss in the prawns to cook until nicely coloured. Remove from heat and set aside.

Turn the heat to medium-low, and add the garlic, shallots and chilli to the same wok. Fry until the mixture is fragrant before stirring in the XO sauce. Add the dough strips and drizzle in 1–2 tablespoonfuls of water if they are clumpy, stirring until they soften and separate. Season with light and dark soy sauces, salt and pepper to taste.

Push everything in the wok to one side and add the eggs to the empty side. Let them set for a moment before using the spatula to scramble them and mix well with the noodles. Continue to stir-fry until everything is nicely charred and fragrant. If you need to loosen things up a little, just drizzle in a little water.

When you're happy with the texture and char, toss in the bean sprouts and quickly stir-fry for 20 seconds. Add the century egg, if using, and throw in the prawns. Toss together, taste and adjust seasoning as desired. Garnish with cilantro and serve with sriracha or other chilli sauce on the side.

TOM YUM SPAGHETTI

This is tom yum goong, done up Italiano-style with tomato sauce, basil, parmigiano and twirled with some pasta. You basically pound the aromatics characteristic of tom yum into a paste which then flavours your tomato sauce. This, along with oil that has been infused with prawn shells (why not, since we already have them on hand?), is used to build a fragrant base for the pasta. I know there's some rule about seafood and cheese not mixing, ever, but damn, grate some parmigiano over this tomato sauce and you'll know why rules are meant to be broken.

SERVES 2–3

8–10 medium or large prawns, or as many as desired, heads and shells removed and reserved

80 ml canola oil

4–5 kaffir lime leaves

1 1/2 Tbsp *nam prik pao* (Thai chilli paste), available at Thai supermarkets

484 g canned tomatoes

1 1/2 Tbsp fish sauce

250 g dried spaghetti

2 Tbsp lime juice

Basil or cilantro for garnishing

Grated Parmigiano-Reggiano to taste (optional)

TOM YUM PASTE

1 stalk lemongrass

2 bird's eye chillies

4 shallots or 1 large onion, peeled

10 g galangal, peeled

Continuing the Feast

Nam prik pao is used in Salmon Belly on a Bed of Herbs (p 48), Creamy Tom Yum Goong (p 112) and Vegan Tom Yum (p 130).

Galangal is used in Seared Snapper (p 40), Laab Meatballs (p 64), Creamy Tom Yum Goong (p 112), Vegetarian Pho (p 118) and Vegan Tom Yum (p 130).

Devein the prawns by making a slit down the back and removing the black vein. Wash the prawns thoroughly and set aside.

Prepare the tom yum paste. For the lemongrass, bruise it with the back of a knife, remove the tough outer leaves and use only the tender inner stems of the bottom half. If using a mortar and pestle, pound the aromatics — lemongrass, chillies, shallots and galangal — together to form a rough paste. If not, individually mince them finely and combine, or blitz with a food processor.

Heat the oil over medium-low heat in a large Dutch oven or pot, then add the reserved prawn heads and shells. Using the back of a wooden spoon, squish the heads down to help release the flavourful prawn juices. When the prawn heads and shells turn light golden, strain and discard the shells, keeping only the precious orange-red liquid.

Over low heat in the same pot, add the tom yum paste and lime leaves, then fry for a couple of minutes, until the paste softens and releases even more flavour into the oil. (You know it's gonna be good!)

Add the *nam prik pao* and stir for about 20 seconds before adding the tomatoes. Stir in the fish sauce, cover and let simmer over low heat for about 15 minutes.

Meanwhile, prep the spaghetti. Add to rapidly boiling and heavily salted water and cook for 2 minutes less than the time given in the instructions. Drain the spaghetti and reserve the cooking liquid.

Add the spaghetti and prawns to the sauce and turn the heat to low. Cook together for 1 minute or so. If the sauce is too dry, add a splash of pasta cooking liquid.

Switch off the heat and stir in the lime juice. Taste and adjust seasoning as desired. Garnish with more lime leaves, cilantro or basil, and grate the cheese over. Portion into individual serving plates or eat straight from the pot.

I know there's some rule about seafood and cheese not mixing, ever, but damn, grate some parmigiano over this tomato sauce and you'll know why rules are meant to be broken.

SOMEN WITH CLAMS IN JINHUA HAM DASHI

This light stock is the work of moments. You make a *dashi* with the addition of prized Chinese ingredients like Jinhua ham and dried scallops, and then flavour it with the clams, ginger, spring onion and some Chinese wine. If you can't find the ham, feel free to use bacon in its place.

SERVES 2

500 g clams

1 Tbsp sesame oil

25 g ginger, peeled, cut into slices and lightly bruised

2 stalks spring onions, thinly sliced

1 Tbsp Shaoxing wine

1 Tbsp dried goji berries

100 g dried somen noodles

DASHI

20 g Jinhua ham

10 g dried scallops

8 g kombu

700 ml water

Continuing the Feast

Dried goji berries are used in Sesame Chicken Somen (p 117) and Trio-Egg Spinach (p 128).

Jinhua ham is used in Superior Stock (p 124).

Dried scallops are used in Radish Cake (p 82), Superior Stock (p 124) and Premium Udon Soup (p 134).

Kombu is used in Vietnamese Chicken Porridge (p 88), Fish Congee (p 91), Sesame Chicken Somen (p 117), Superior Stock (p 124) and Vegan Tom Yum (p 130).

Place all the *dashi* ingredients in a large saucepan and bring to a simmer. When it begins to simmer, remove the kombu immediately. Cover the stock and leave to continue simmering for 20–30 minutes.

In the meantime, start prepping the clams. Place the clams in a large pot of water and scrub them clean, ensuring that there is no trace of dirt or residue on their shells. Transfer to another pot filled with iced water and leave to soak for 1 hour, refreshing the water every 15 minutes. Discard any empty open shells and any grit extracted. Drain and set aside.

When the stock is ready, it's time to make the soup. Heat the oil in a large stockpot over medium-low heat. Add the ginger and spring onions and stir-fry until fragrant, about 30–40 seconds.

Add the stock, Shaoxing wine and goji berries. Leave to simmer for about 10 minutes, letting the flavours mix and develop.

While the soup simmers, cook the somen noodles according to the package instructions. Drain and set aside.

Add the clams, turn the heat to high and cook until the clams open. Taste and adjust seasoning as desired. It's likely you won't need to add any salty element cause the ham, scallops and clams all bring their own saltiness to the dish.

To serve, pile the noodles into a bowl and ladle the soup and clams over.

PEPPERY GLASS NOODLES WITH PRAWNS

This is one of my family's favourite dishes. Here, both white and black peppers are incorporated for their nuances in fragrance and warmth. The peppercorns and aromatics like garlic, ginger and cilantro roots are all pounded to release their flavours before being sautéed in rendered prawn oil. We also marinate the glass noodles in seasoned stock beforehand to ensure all that flavour seeps to their core. After a brief cooking spell, the noodles will absorb all that peppery sauce, becoming glossy and slicked with flavour. I guarantee that this will be an absolute treat for your guests!

SERVES 3–4

160 g glass noodles

250 ml chicken or seafood stock, unsalted

2 Tbsp oyster sauce

2 Tbsp fish sauce

1 Tbsp light soy sauce

2 tsp dark soy sauce

1 tsp sesame oil

1 1/2 tsp white sugar

300 g prawns, about 6–8

1 1/2 tsp black peppercorns

1 1/2 tsp white peppercorns

6 cloves garlic, peeled

3–4 cilantro roots (substitute with cilantro stems if unavailable)

50 g old ginger, peeled and sliced

2 1/2 Tbsp canola oil or lard

Spring onions and cilantro for garnishing, chopped

Continuing the Feast
Cilantro root is used in Seared Snapper (p 40). The leftover cilantro sprigs can be used for garnishing many dishes.

Soak the noodles in room temperature water for 10 minutes to soften. While the noodles soak, combine the stock, oyster sauce, fish sauce, light and dark soy sauces, sesame oil and sugar in another bowl. When the noodles are softened, drain and place in the seasoned stock to marinate for 20–30 minutes.

Prep the prawns by trimming the feelers and removing the black vein down their backs. Wash and dry the prawns thoroughly.

Let's move on to the peppercorns and aromatics. Use a mortar and pestle or a coffee grinder to ground the peppercorns — if doing it by hand, it won't end up like a fine powder and that's totally all right. Bruise the garlic, cilantro roots and ginger lightly to help release the flavours. You can do this with a mortar and pestle or the back of a knife. Be careful not to overdo this — we don't want a paste here.

Add the canola oil to a claypot or Dutch oven over high heat. When the oil is hot, add the prawns and sear on both sides. Stand back with your longest tongs and be prepared for the oil splatter. It will be a little scary, but it must be done for the great prawn flavour. The prawns don't need to be entirely through at this point, so remove and set aside once they are seared.

Keeping the prawn-y oil in the pot, turn the heat to low and add the garlic, cilantro roots and ginger. Sauté until fragrant and softened, then add the ground peppercorns. Stir-fry briefly for 20–30 seconds, before pouring in the stock and noodles. Give it a good stir and clamp the lid shut. Cook for 2 minutes, then use a pair of tongs to stir and ensure even cooking. Replace the lid and let it cook for another 1–2 minutes, until the noodles soak up all that delicious sauce.

Taste the noodles for texture and seasoning, then adjust as desired. Stir in the prawns and let them heat through. When the prawns are just cooked, toss in the spring onions and cilantro, switch off the heat and cover the pot again. Let the spring onions wilt slightly to release their flavours, then you're ready to serve!

The peppercorns and other aromatics like garlic, ginger and cilantro roots are all pounded before being sautéed in prawn oil to produce a peppery sauce.

SOUPY STUFF

—

" *For me, a good bowl of pho will always make me happy.* **"**

– ANTHONY BOURDAIN

CREAMY TOM YUM GOONG WITH INSTANT NOODZ

Tom yum goong, or tom yum with prawns, is undisputedly the most popular iteration of this famous hot and sour soup. In Thailand, you can get two distinct styles: clear or creamy. They typically add evaporated milk or coconut milk to turn the fiery hue of the soup to a more muted orange, dotted with droplets of oil. To improve the flavour of the soup, I use the prawn shells and heads to make a quick prawn stock. Once that's done, it is the work of mere minutes to infuse all the aromatics in the soup. Serve with some Mama instant noodles or glass noodles to sop up the mouthwatering and piquant broth.

SERVES 4

2 stalks lemongrass

3– 5 bird's eye chillies, or to taste, cut into chunks

3–4 slices galangal

8–10 kaffir lime leaves

200 g mushrooms (use whichever type you enjoy in soups)

1–2 tomatoes or 10–12 small cherry tomatoes, cut into chunks

55 ml evaporated milk

65 ml fish sauce

2 tsp *nam prik pao* (Thai chilli paste)

$1/2$ tsp white sugar

12–14 prawns, peeled and deveined, with shells and heads reserved

70 ml lime juice

4 packets Mama noodles or other instant noodles of your choice, seasoning discarded

Cilantro for garnishing

PRAWN STOCK

Shells and heads from 12–14 prawns

1 Tbsp canola oil

1.3 litres water

Continuing the Feast
Galangal is used in Seared Snapper (p 40), Laab Meatballs (p 64), Tom Yum Spaghetti (p 104), Vegetarian Pho (p 118) and Vegan Tom Yum (p 130).

Nam prik pao is used in Salmon Belly on a Bed of Herbs (p 48), Tom Yum Spaghetti (p 104) and Vegan Tom Yum (p 130).

To make a quick prawn stock, dry the prawn shells and heads thoroughly. In a Dutch oven or large stockpot, heat the canola oil over medium-high heat. Add the prawn shells and heads, frying thoroughly until they take on a beautiful reddish colour and smell roasted. Add water to deglaze the pot, then reduce the heat to low and simmer, uncovered, for 15 minutes. Strain prawn stock and set aside. You'll need 1 litre, so if you don't have sufficient stock, top up with enough water to make 1 litre.

Let's now prep the aromatics for the soup. For the lemongrass, cut off the bottom end and remove the tough outer leaves. Use the back of a knife or a mortar and pestle to bruise the lemongrass and help release its flavour. Cut the chillies into small chunks.

Heat the stock in a pot over low heat and add the lemongrass, chillies and galangal. Scrunch up the lime leaves to release their aroma and add them to the pot. Toss in the mushrooms and tomatoes, then allow everything to infuse for about 5 minutes.

Now, time for seasoning it: add the evaporated milk, fish sauce, *nam prik pao* and sugar. Tip in the prawns and once they are cooked, switch off the heat.

Finally, add the lime juice. Taste and adjust the seasoning as desired. The soup should be spicy and sour, followed by a back note of saltiness and rounded off by sweetness.

If using another brand of instant noodles, you'll need to cook them first according to the package instrucstions. The amazing thing about using Mama noodles (which are delicious as a crunchy snack by the way) is that you don't have to cook them — if you boil the noodles separately before adding them, they'll be overcooked and soggy! So here we just let the aromatic hot and sour soup seep into the cakes of noodles to soften them. They'll be just right in a few minutes. By the time the bowls of noodle soup are set on your table, they would have reached the perfect consistency.

Garnish with cilantro, if desired.

SMOKY CHICKEN SOUP WITH BLISTERED GRAPES AND JACKFRUIT

This was inspired by a soup I had at Paste, helmed by Chef Bongkoch "Bee" Satongun. She reimagined a traditional Thai soup that had flavours and textures that completely blew me away. It was a punchy, smoky and sour soup with a playful sweetness. I dug into the bowl and unearthed goodies like slices of fried garlic, tomatoes, jackfruit seeds and this flavour bomb of pork leg, cooked and charred in all the right spots. But if you'd like to eat that perfect pork leg nestled in the soup, head to Paste in Bangkok, because I've made a home (and sanity) friendly version. In this version, you'll get shreds of dark chicken meat that's also part of the stock-making. I'd get too grumpy if I had to make a stock, and stew AND fry pork leg. So I pick my battles.

SERVES 2–4 AS A STARTER

8 shallots, peeled

4–5 jackfruit segments, seeds intact

8–10 grapes or cherry tomatoes

1 Tbsp fish sauce

Salt to taste

15 g tamarind paste, combined with 2 Tbsp water

Ground black pepper to serve

Cilantro for garnishing

Crispy fried garlic for garnishing

Garlic oil for garnishing

ROAST CHICKEN STOCK

4 Tbsp canola oil

2 whole chicken legs, skin and bone intact

600 g chicken bones

Salt to taste

Ground black pepper to taste

2.5 litres water

Continuing the Feast
Jackfruit is used in Jackfruit Kra Pow (p 80).

Tamarind paste is used in Asian Slaw (p 28).

First, we'll make the stock. Preheat the oven to 220°C. Rub the oil all over the chicken legs and bones, then set aside the bones in a stockpot. Salt and pepper the chicken legs before placing on a tray and roasting for 20–25 minutes, until golden brown. Transfer roasted chicken legs to the stockpot, add the water, then simmer over low heat for 1.5–2 hours.

Strain the stock and reserve the chicken bones as well as the chicken legs. You'll only need 800 ml of this stock, so cool and freeze the leftover for other uses. Shred the chicken leg meat into largish chunks and set aside.

Preheat the oven to 220°C. Place the shallots and chicken bones on a tray and roast for 5 minutes until nicely charred. Discard the bones and set aside the shallots while you prepare the jackfruit. Shred the jackfruit flesh or cut into chunks (you don't want them too thin), reserving the seeds.

In a large saucepan, add the stock, roasted shallots, jackfruit flesh and seeds, grapes and fish sauce. Let simmer for 5–10 minutes before seasoning with salt to taste. Add the chicken chunks and follow by the tamarind water to taste. The amount would depend on sourness of the tamarind paste. The soup should be predominantly sour and punchy, held together by a melody of subtle sweetness. Adjust the seasoning to your liking.

Portion into individual bowls and garnish with a cracking of black pepper, cilantro and crispy fried garlic. Drizzle with garlic oil and serve.

This was inspired by a soup I had at Paste, helmed by Chef Bongkoch "Bee" Satongun. She reimagined a traditional Thai soup that had flavours and textures that completely blew me away.

SESAME CHICKEN SOMEN NOODZ

This is a version of a dish that's evolved from the sesame chicken recipe found in my first book. I first shared a soupier version of the original recipe online and paired it with some silky somen noodles — and people who made it started tagging me and saying how simple and delicious this was to make. The version you see here is further adapted from the one online. I've used only chicken legs here and added a square of kombu to soak with the dried mushrooms, essentially making a mushroom *dashi* for the base, which lends more depth of flavour to the soup.

SERVES 4

4 whole chicken legs, bone-in, skin removed

1 Tbsp oyster sauce

1 Tbsp light soy sauce

5 Tbsp sesame oil

60 g old ginger, peeled and sliced into large chunks

Enough water to just cover the chicken

3 Tbsp Shaoxing wine

1/2 teapsoon salt

2 Tbsp dried goji berries

200 g dried somen noodles

MUSHROOM DASHI

8 dried Chinese mushrooms

5-cm cube kombu

500 ml water

Continuing the Feast

Dried goji berries are used in Somen with Clams (p 107) and Trio-Egg Spinach (p 128).

Kombu is used in Vietnamese Chicken Porridge (p 88), Fish Congee (p 91), Somen with Clams (p 107), Superior Stock (p 124) and Vegan Tom Yum (p 130).

Start off with the mushroom *dashi*. Place the mushrooms, kombu and water together in a bowl and leave to soak for at least a couple of hours. You can also leave this to soak overnight, covered, in the refrigerator. When ready to use, strain the *dashi* and reserve the mushrooms.

Season the chicken legs with the oyster sauce, soy sauce and 1 tablespoonful of sesame oil. Set aside for 10–15 minutes as you prep the rest of the ingredients.

Lightly bruise the ginger chunks. Cut the reserved mushrooms into large chunks. Keep the bowl of mushroom *dashi* at hand.

Heat a large Dutch oven or claypot over medium-low heat and add 4 tablespoonfuls of sesame oil. Toss in the ginger and stir-fry over until fragrant, about 40 seconds. Add the mushrooms and crank the heat up to high. Allow them to take on some colour before tipping in the chicken legs and the marinade. Give a good stir to make sure everything is evenly coated. Pour in the mushroom *dashi* and add enough water to just cover the chicken. Add the Shaoxing wine and salt, then let everything come to a boil.

Once it reaches a boil, turn the heat down to low, clamp the lid on and let everything simmer for 40–50 minutes, until the chicken is tender. You need time for the legs to stew to tenderness, but start checking at the 40-minute mark and let it go on a little longer if it's not as fall-apart tender as you'd like. If the water level drops too much, just add more water.

Finally, when the chicken is tender, add the goji berries and let simmer for 5 minutes more. Taste and adjust seasoning as desired with more soy sauce or salt.

Meanwhile, cook the noodles according to the package instructions. Portion into 4 bowls and ladle the sauce, mushrooms and goji berries over. Top each bowl with a chicken leg.

VEGETARIAN PHO (PHO CHAY)

Joycelyn Shu, a culinary instructor and writer, has had a long-held fascination with the vegetarian foodways of South East Asia. In particular, she's passionate about the Vietnamese noodle soup, *pho chay* (vegetarian pho). While it is relatively easy to find a good bowl of *pho bo* (beef pho) or *pho gà* (chicken pho), it's far more difficult to get your hands on a bowl of great *pho chay*. The solution is clear: make it at home, with a vegetable stock brewed from scratch. A great *pho chay* broth, the kind you want to lick every last drop of, takes as much time and effort to craft as a meat-based broth. There are no shortcuts to get this broth with flavours teased from root vegetables, dried mushrooms, a cast of warm spices and charred aromatics. This is a recipe that Joycelyn has been refining for years now; she hopes you will like it. If you're pressed for time, you can choose to make just a few of the toppings.

SERVES 4

RICH VEGETABLE STOCK

15 dried Chinese mushrooms, preferably flower shiitake (*hua gu*)

Water as needed, at room temperature

4 Tbsp neutral vegetable oil

4 stalks celery, ends trimmed, thinly sliced

2 carrots, peeled, trimmed and thinly sliced

2 onions, peeled, trimmed and thinly sliced

4 cloves garlic, peeled, trimmed and smashed

1 1/2 tsp fine sea salt

400 g fresh shiitake mushrooms or portobello mushrooms, diced and stems removed

BROTH

1 Tbsp whole black peppercorns

1 Tbsp coriander seeds

6 star anise

6 cloves

2 sticks cinnamon

2 onions, peeled, trimmed and quartered

1 head garlic, papery outer layer peeled off, top trimmed to expose flesh

7.5-cm knob young ginger, unpeeled, cleaned and halved

2 stalks scallions, white portion only, trimmed and smashed

We begin with the rich vegetable stock. Place the dried mushrooms and 2 litres water in a bowl. Cover with cling film and soak for 12–24 hours at room temperature. Strain and reserve the soaking liquid. Trim and discard the mushroom stems.

Heat the vegetable oil in a large heavy-bottomed pot over medium-high heat. Add the celery, carrots, onions, garlic and salt, then sauté for about 10 minutes, stirring occasionally, until wilted and slightly golden.

Add the fresh mushrooms as well as the soaked dried mushrooms. Sauté for another 5 minutes, or until the fresh mushrooms have released their juices. Add the reserved soaking liquid and 2 litres water. Bring to the boil over high heat before turning the heat to low and simmering for about 1 hour with the pot partially covered.

Let the stock cool slightly before straining through a fine-mesh sieve. Do this in batches and press firmly on the vegetables to extract as much flavour as possible. Pick out the dried mushrooms and discard the other vegetables. To get rid of any grit, strain the stock a second time through a fine-mesh sieve lined with a muslin cloth. Set aside 4 tablespoonfuls for the braised mushrooms and return the remaining stock to the pot.

Now, to make the broth. In a small frying pan over low heat, toast the peppercorns, coriander seeds, star anise, cloves and cinnamon together until aromatic. Set toasted spices aside.

In a large frying pan over medium heat, char the cut sides of the onions, garlic, ginger and scallions until deeply caramelised, blistered in spots and aromatic.

1 portion rich vegetable stock,
   setting aside 4 Tbsp for the
   braised mushrooms

7 stalks lemongrass, trimmed and
   spliced in half

6 slices galangal

2 dried red chillies

8 kaffir lime leaves

1 Tbsp raw cane sugar, or to taste

4 Tbsp light soy sauce, or to taste

1 tsp fine sea salt, or to taste

BRAISED MUSHROOMS

15 cooked dried Chinese
   mushrooms, from making the
   rich vegetable stock

1 Tbsp Shaoxing wine

1 Tbsp raw cane sugar, or to taste

4 Tbsp light soy sauce, or to taste

4 Tbsp rich vegetable stock

**SMOKY KING OYSTER
MUSHROOMS AND TEMPEH**

4 Tbsp light soy sauce

4 Tbsp maple syrup

1 Tbsp liquid smoke seasoning

4 Tbsp Shaoxing wine

800 g large king oyster mushroom,
   trimmed, cut into 0.5-cm thick
   slices

225 g tempeh, cut into 0.5-cm thick
   slices

Toasted white sesame oil for
   searing

In a large pot, add charred aromatics, toasted spices and vegetable stock. Throw in the lemongrass, galangal, dried chillies and lime leaves. Bring to the boil over high heat before turning the heat to low and simmering for about 30 minutes with the pot partially covered.

Strain the broth and season with sugar, soy sauce and salt, adding more to taste as desired. Leave to cool and store in an airtight container for up to 5 days.

For the braised mushrooms, cut the mushrooms into 1-cm thick slices. Combine with the Shaoxing wine, sugar, soy sauce and stock in a small saucepan over medium-low heat and braise with the pot partially covered until the juices have reduced to a syrupy consistency. Adjusting the seasoning to taste if necessary.

For the smoky king oyster mushrooms and tempeh, combine the soy sauce, maple syrup, liquid smoke seasoning and Shaoxing wine to make a marinade. Coat the mushrooms with 5 tablespoonfuls of marinade. Separately, coat the tempeh with 2–4 tablespoonfuls of marinade. Cover mushrooms and tempeh with cling film and leave to marinate at room temperature for 1–2 hours.

Drain the mushroom and tempeh slices and pat dry. Heat a drizzle of sesame oil in a non-stick skillet over medium-high heat. In a single layer, fry the mushroom and tempeh slices on both sides until crispy and lightly caramelized. Do this in batches, wiping the skillet clean and adding more sesame oil as necessary before each batch. Deglaze the skillet with leftover marinade if you would like the mushroom and tempeh pieces to taste more assertively of the marinade's flavours.

VEGETABLE SLICES

2 carrots, peeled, trimmed and cut into 0.5-cm slices

500 g Chinese white radish, peeled, trimmed, quartered and cut into 0.5-cm slices

TO SERVE

240 g dried flat rice noodles

A large handful of bean sprouts, blanched

1 block deep-fried firm tofu (*tau kwa*), cut into 0.5-cm slabs

1 onion, peeled, trimmed and thinly sliced, then soaked in water for 15 minutes and drained

1 red chilli, thinly sliced

2 large limes, halved

2 stalks spring onions, trimmed and thinly sliced

Large handfuls of fresh herbs such as coriander, mint or Thai basil

Crispy fried shallots for garnishing

Crispy fried garlic for garnishing

Continuing the Feast

Coriander seeds are used in Chicken Pho (p 122).

Cinnamon sticks and star anise are used in Tea-Smoked Duck Legs (p 52), Braised Beef Brisket (p 63) and Chilli Beef Noodz (p 98).

Galangal is used in Seared Snapper (p 40), Laab Meatballs (p 64), Tom Yum Spaghetti (p 104), Creamy Tom Yum Goong (p 112) and Vegan Tom Yum (p 130).

For the vegetable slices, bring the broth to the boil, then add the carrot and radish. Turn the heat to low and simmer for 10–15 minutes until the vegetables are tender (but not mushy). Use a skimmer to gently lift the vegetables out to set aside.

To serve, cook the rice noodles according to the package instructions. Portion into serving bowls and ladle the broth over the noodles. Top with braised mushrooms, smoky king oyster mushroom and tempeh slices, and vegetable slices. Add bean sprouts, tofu slabs and onion slices. Garnish with cut chilli, limes, spring onions, herbs and crispy fried shallots and garlic.

If desired, serve with hoisin and sriracha as dipping sauces. You can also serve this with marinated drunken eggs.

CHICKEN PHO (PHO GA)

A tangle of herbs, a squirt of citrusy lime juice and bright red slices of chillies cut through the chicken soup, adding freshness, tang and spice. It was until I tasted chicken pho in Vietnam that I truly started to appreciate the dish as more than just a plain noodle soup; it's the full works all coming together. In Vietnam, the herbs are not just for mere garnish; they're a panoply showcasing the various local herbs and vegetables that grow in abundance there. Wherever you are, use whatever herbs and tangle of veggies you can get your hands on! The key is that each bite should taste light, refreshing and nourishing.

SERVES 4

1 yellow onion, unpeeled

30 g ginger, unpeeled

2 tsp coriander seeds

1 star anise

1 whole chicken, about 1.2 kg, head removed

2 litres water

1 tsp white sugar

2 tsp salt + more to taste

2 tsp fish sauce + more to taste

250 g dried pho noodles (I used rice noodles with turmeric here but any flat rice noodles for pho will do)

TO SERVE

1 yellow onion, peeled and thinly sliced

A bunch of bean sprouts

Large red chillies, sliced

A large bunch of herbs (use a mix of Vietnamese basil or sweet basil, mint, cilantro, sawtooth coriander and spring onions)

Limes, cut into halves

Continuing the Feast

Coriander seeds are used in Vegetarian Pho (p 118).

Star anise is used in Tea-Smoked Duck Legs (p 52), Braised Beef Brisket (p 63), Chilli Beef Noodz (p 98) and Vegetarian Pho (p 118).

Begin with making the soup. Preheat the oven to 240°C. Place the whole onion and knob of ginger on a foil-lined baking tray and let them char in the oven, about 20 minutes. They should be properly blackened — no place for restraint here. You could also do this in a dry saucepan over high heat on the stove.

Toast the coriander seeds and star anise in a saucepan over medium heat until fragrant. Set aside.

Place the chicken in a stockpot or claypot. Add the water, which should just cover the chicken, followed by the coriander seeds and star anise. Peel and discard the blackened skins before placing the onion and ginger in the pot. You could also leave the skins on for a darker soup. Add the sugar, salt and fish sauce.

Simmer everything over the lowest possible heat. This is key to keeping the pho soup clear and light. Constantly skim away any scum that rises to the surface as the soup simmers for 1.5 hours.

Remove the chicken to let it cool before deboning and shredding the meat into chunks. Strain the soup using a cheesecloth or fine-mesh sieve and return to the pot.

Before cooking the noodles, prepare the onion slices for garnishing. Soak them in a bowl of iced water to get rid of the spicy bite.

Cook the noodles according to the package instructions. When the noodles are done, drain, rinse under running water and portion into serving bowls.

For each bowl, top with some sliced onions, bean sprouts and a mound of chicken meat. Make sure that each bowl has a good mix of both white and dark meat from the breast and the legs.

Warm up the stock so that it's piping hot when you ladle it into each bowl.

To serve, pile the chillies, herbs, additional bean sprouts and limes on a plate for your diners to customise their own bowl of soup to taste. I'd recommend tearing the herbs and adding them to the broth as they eat, as well as that squeeze of lime and some chilli slices. This is ESSENTIAL to pho!

A tangle of herbs, a squirt of citrusy lime juice and bright red slices of chillies cut through the chicken soup, adding freshness, tang and spice.

SUPERIOR STOCK

I take a page from Japanese ramen stock by adding a square of kombu to my traditional Chinese superior stock. This is the stock you get when dining out at a fancy Chinese restaurant. It's a compound stock with the luxurious addition of Jinhua ham and dried scallops, cooked slowly over many hours until it results in liquid gold. You'll get a clear, complex and rich stock at your disposal for luxing up anything from stir-fries to stews, soups or fancy banquet dishes... you name it. It takes a fair bit of time to simmer, but you don't really have to do much aside from the occasional skimming. My advice: make a double batch to freeze in portions. You've just made a fancy, restaurant-quality superior stock at home!

SERVES 10

750 g pork bones

500 g chicken bones

3 slices ginger

A bunch of spring onions, tied into a knot

1 tsp whole white peppercorns

75 g dried scallops

65 g Jinhua ham

5-cm cube kombu (optional)

4 litres water

Continuing the Feast
Jinhua ham is used in Somen with Clams (p 107).

Kombu is used in Vietnamese Chicken Porridge (p 88), Fish Congee (p 91), Somen with Clams (p 107), Sesame Chicken Somen (p 117) and Vegan Tom Yum (p 130).

Superior stock is used in Wontons in Superior Stock (p 127) and Trio-Egg Spinach (p 128).

Rinse the pork bones and chicken bones before placing them in a large pot. Cover the bones with water and bring to the boil. Let this boil vigorously for 10–15 minutes so that the scum rises to the surface. Drain to extract the pork and chicken pieces and rinse well again.

In a large stockpot, place the rinsed bones, ginger, spring onions, peppercorns, dried scallops, ham and kombu. Add the water, making sure it covers everything, then cover and bring to a very gentle simmer over the lowest heat.

Let simmer for at least 4–6 hours, occasionally skimming away any scum that rises to the surface. You could also use one of those scum absorbing sheets to do so.

Strain the stock through a cheesecloth or fine-mesh sieve. Leave to cool before using or portioning to store in the freezer. You've made a beautifully clear superior stock!

WONTONS IN SUPERIOR STOCK

Chinese food is all about texture and mouthfeel. The silky smooth skin of a wonton gives way to the bouncy, slightly crunchy textured filling. There are several things that contribute to this ideal texture — the way the pork and prawns are treated, and the various add-ins like dried fungus and water chestnuts. These wontons taste luxurious floating in some superior stock, which is already so flavourful that you'll only need a smidgen of salt as seasoning, if you're so inclined.

MAKES 35-40 WONTONS

1 packet of wonton wrappers, about 40 sheets

Superior stock as desired (p 124)

FILLING

200 g prawns meat, chopped into chunks

1 tsp Chinese rice wine or Shaoxing wine

2 tsp sesame oil

Ground white pepper to taste

2 pieces dried black fungus, soaked for 30 minutes

100 g minced pork

1/2 tsp salt

2 stalks spring onions, minced into thin rings

1/4 tsp grated ginger

3 tsp light soy sauce

1 Tbsp egg white

1/2 tsp white sugar

1 tsp cornstarch or potato starch

2 water chestnuts, peeled and chopped into cubes

2 Tbsp water or stock

> **Continuing the Feast**
> *Dried black fungus is used in Vegan Tom Yum (p 130).*
>
> *Superior stock is used in Trio-Egg Spinach (p 128).*

For the filling, we'll start by prepping the prawns. Chop them into tiny chunks (you want to retain some texture) and drizzle in Chinese wine, 1 teaspoonful of sesame oil and pepper. Mix well, cover and set aside in the refrigerator.

Drain the fungus and remove the tough woody stems. Roll up the fungus and slice into thin strips. Set aside.

Combine the minced pork and salt in a large mixing bowl, then mix well using your hands or a pair of chopsticks, vigorously working the mixture. You could also pick up the clump of minced meat in one hand and slap it back into the bowl a couple of times. This helps to denature the proteins, and the meat will lighten in colour and start to feel sticky.

Once the pork is lightened, add the spring onions, ginger, soy sauce, 1 teaspoonful of sesame oil, egg white, sugar and cornstarch. Mix everything well until it is combined. Now, add the prawn mixture, black fungus and water chestnuts, and mix in evenly. Cook a small piece of the filling in a small pot of water or the microwave to taste for seasoning. Adjust to taste if necessary.

Before wrapping the wontons, have at your disposal the wonton wrappers, a small bowl of water (for sealing the edges) and the filling. To start, dollop some filling in the centre of a square wonton wrapper. Dab your fingertips in the bowl of water and moisten two adjoining sides of the square. Fold the other sides over so that a triangle forms, then seal tightly. Take one end of the triangle and fold it towards the centre. Repeat with the other side so that the wonton looks like it is giving itself a hug. Moisten with water to seal. Well, you're basically just sealing some meat and prawn filling in dumpling wrappers — do it whichever way that comes naturally to you! Repeat until the filling is used up.

At this point, you have your little wontons ready. You can either freeze them for future use or start prepping them for this dish. Bring a pot of water to the boil. Add the wontons to the rapidly boiling water and cook until they float to the top and the wonton skins turn translucent. Drain and set aside.

In another pot, bring the superior stock to the boil. Taste and adjust the seasoning with a pinch of salt if desired. Add wontons and heat briefly before ladling into serving bowls.

TRIO-EGG SPINACH IN SUPERIOR STOCK

This dish is a sight to behold. Vibrant emerald greens are dotted with bright orange-red goji berries and the translucent brown-black jelly cubes of century egg, swimming amidst swirling clouds of egg. Sometimes, I top the soup with crispy fried whitebait. If you prefer this as a soupier dish, use a larger amount of stock. If you want to keep this more vegetable-focused, feel free to reduce the stock and seasoning.

SERVES 2–4 AS A SIDE DISH

2 eggs

1 century egg

1 salted egg

1 Tbsp sesame oil

3–4 cloves garlic, peeled

650 ml superior stock (p 124) or any other stock you prefer

1 Tbsp dried goji berries

1/2 tsp white sugar

1/4–1/2 tsp salt, or to taste

Ground white pepper to taste

250 g Chinese round spinach or red amaranth leaves, cleaned and rinsed, roots trimmed

1 Tbsp Shaoxing wine (optional)

CRISPY FRIED WHITEBAIT (OPTIONAL)

4 Tbsp neutral vegetable oil

4 Tbsp whitebait

> **Continuing the Feast**
> *Century egg is used in Porridge Kueh Stir-Fry (p 102).*
>
> *Dried goji berries are used in Somen with Clams (p 107) and Sesame Chicken Somen (p 117).*
>
> *Superior stock is used in Wontons in Superior Stock (p 127).*

In a small bowl, whisk the eggs and set aside. Peel and dice the century egg. If the salted egg is uncooked, add it to a pot of boiling water and boil until fully cooked. Leave to cool before peeling and dicing the salted egg.

In a medium saucepan or claypot, heat the oil over low heat. Add the whole garlic cloves and fry until the sides of the garlic are light golden brown before adding the stock.

Toss in your goji berries, sugar, salt and white pepper, then let the stock come to a simmer. When it starts to simmer, add your spinach or amaranth leaves and let them wilt in the hot soup. As they cook, add the century egg and salted egg. After about 30 seconds, taste for saltiness and adjust the seasoning as desired. If you intend to top the dish with some crispy fried whitebait, remember that it will add a salty note too.

Drizzle in the beaten eggs slowly, stirring the soup as you do so. Splash in the Shaoxing wine and switch off the heat immediately.

Transfer the vegetables and eggs into a dish and ladle over the flavourful broth. Serve piping hot.

If choosing to top with crispy fried whitebait, prepare the topping before making the dish. Heat about 4 tablespoonfuls of vegetable oil in a saucepan over medium heat. Add the whitebait and reduce the heat to low. Fry until evenly golden brown, then set aside to cool on paper towels.

VEGAN TOM YUM UDON

The usual suspects — aromatics like lemongrass, kaffir lime leaves, galangal and bird's eye chillies — can be found here. Instead of fish sauce, we use light soy sauce here to keep things vegan. To add depth of flavour, I've added some charred shallots for smoky sweetness and *nam prik pao*, a Thai chilli paste that also provides a touch of oil to this lean soup. You can find this condiment in any Thai grocery shop, and you can use it in other dishes like tom yum spaghetti or creamy tom yum goong with instant noodz. You can add in any vegetables or mushrooms you'd like, so go crazy and toss in your picks. The chewy udon noodles soak up the spicy and sour soup marvellously. Feel free to add a dash of MSG if you're so inclined.

SERVES 2

4 shallots, peeled

2 stalks lemongrass

1–2 bird's eye chillies, or to taste

8 slices galangal

6 kaffir lime leaves, torn

300 g fresh udon noodles

2 dried black fungus, soaked in water

200 g mushrooms (use a mix of your choice, such as enoki, shiitake, shimeiji, etc.), cleaned

1 Tbsp *nam prik pao* (Thai chilli paste)

2 Tbsp light soy sauce

8–10 sugar snap peas

2 Tbsp lime juice, or to taste

A pinch of salt or MSG (optional)

Cilantro for garnishing

Crispy fried shallots for garnishing

MUSHROOM DASHI

3 dried Chinese mushrooms

10 g kombu

1.2 litres water

50 g white Chinese radish (optional)

Continuing the Feast

Galangal is used in Seared Snapper (p 40), Laab Meatballs (p 64), Tom Yum Spaghetti (p 104) Creamy Tom Yum Goong (p 112) and Vegetarian Pho (p 118).

Dried black fungus is used in Wontons in Superior Stock (p 127).

MSG is used in Radish Cake (p 82).

Chinese white radish is used in Radish Cake (p 82) and Vegetarian Pho (p 118).

Begin with the mushroom *dashi* by placing the mushrooms, kombu and water in a pot. Leave to soak for 30 minutes before adding the radish, if using, and bringing everything to the boil. Turn the heat to low and simmer for about 30 minutes. Strain, return the *dashi* to the pot and set aside.

Preheat the oven to 220°C. Place the shallots on a lined baking tray and roast until caramelised and charred around the edges.

For the lemongrass, cut off the bottom end and remove the tough outer leaves. Using the back of a knife or a pestle, bruise the lemongrass all over to release its flavour. Cut the chillies into chunks.

Add the shallots, lemongrass, chillies, galangal and lime leaves to the *dashi*, then bring to a simmer. Let the aromatics infuse for 3–5 minutes.

In the meantime, cook the udon according to the package instructions. If using the vacuum-packed ones, they boil up pretty quickly! Drain and portion into two serving bowls.

Drain the soaking fungus and discard the tough stems. Tear into chunks and add to the simmering soup, along with the mushrooms, *nam prik pao* and soy sauce. Simmer for a minute or so, then toss in the sugar snap peas and let them cook through, about 50 seconds. Switch off the heat.

Stir in the lime juice, taste and adjust for seasoning. If it isn't salty enough, add a pinch of salt or MSG. The predominant flavours are spicy and sour, so feel free to add more lime juice or chillies to your preference. Alternatively, serve extra lime wedges and chilli slices on the side.

Ladle soup and the vegetables into the bowls. Garnish with cilantro and crispy fried shallots, then serve hot.

This is a Teochew-style fish porridge, the kind with cooked rice suspended in broth, with the grains plumping up and soaking in all that flavour.

SEAFOOD SOUP WITH RICE

For supper one night in Bangkok, my friend YY and I arrived at an eatery that specialised in fish porridge, the kind with cooked rice suspended in broth, with the grains plumping up and soaking in all that flavour. This is a Teochew-style porridge, which is not surprising as many Teochews have settled down in Thailand. When we entered the eatery, we noticed huge vats filled with obscene amounts of fish bones and prawn shells, a sign of promising things to come. The delicious seafood stock that night came with slices of smooth butter fish, tender squidlets and prawns. So, here's my interpretation of that bowl, done up in the comfort of your own home.

SERVES 4–6

FOR EACH BOWL

350 ml seafood stock

$^1/_2$–$^3/_4$ tsp salt, or to taste

Some prawns and fish slices

120 g cooked jasmine rice

Cilantro for garnishing

Garlic oil for garnishing

Crispy fried garlic for garnishing

Chillies for serving, sliced

Light soy sauce for serving

MARINATED SEAFOOD

12–14 prawns, shells and heads removed and reserved

300 g fish fillet, sliced into chunks

1½ Tbsp Shaoxing wine

1 Tbsp sesame oil

A dash of ground white pepper

SEAFOOD STOCK

200–300 g fish bones (available from a fishmonger, otherwise purchase a whole fish and have it deboned, reserving the bones for this and the meat for marinating)

300 g prawn shells and heads (from marinated prawns)

2 stalks lemongrass, halved (use the leftover top halves of lemongrass from other recipes if you have them)

3 slices ginger, lightly crushed

4 stalks spring onions, tied into a knot

2 litres water

For the seafood stock, wash the fish bones and prawn shells thoroughly by soaking them in iced water for 15 minutes. Drain and rinse them once more before placing in a stockpot. Add the lemongrass, ginger, spring onions and water. Bring to a simmer over low heat and let simmer for an hour.

While the stock is simmering away, marinate your seafood. To the prawns and fish slices, add Shaoxing wine, sesame oil and pepper. Cover with cling film and leave in the refrigerator to marinate.

Strain the stock after it has simmered for an hour. This serves 4–6 people comfortably. Any leftover stock can be kept in the freezer.

To prepare an individual portion, bring 350 ml stock to the boil in a saucepan, then add $^1/_2$ teaspoonful of salt. Add some prawns and cook for 40 seconds before adding some fish slices. When the seafood curls and turns opaque, switch off the heat and adjust for seasoning. Switch off the heat, taste and adjust the seasoning. If it's not salty enough, add more salt or a trickle of fish sauce.

Ladle the soup and seafood into a bowl of rice. Trickle garlic oil and sprinkle crispy fried garlic on top. Garnish with cilantro if desired. Serve with some sliced or minced chillies in light soy sauce to dip the seafood in.

PREMIUM UDON SOUP WITH FISH MAW AND ABALONE

This recipe comes from Caecilia (@Singaporeliciouz on Instagram) who is very generous and giving, which is reflected in her cooking and how she looks after her family. This is a luxe little number she makes whenever there are cans of abalone in the house. She brews it up with some dried seafood and chicken for a bowl of collagen-rich and indulgent noodle soup. You can find dried clams or dried conch in Chinese dried goods stores. This soup is the perfect recipe for using up any leftovers of these prized Chinese delicacies after the Lunar New Year festivities.

SERVES 4

600 g chicken bones

1 chicken breast, bone-in

1 dried clam or dried conch, about 60 g

6–8 dried scallops

2.2 litres water

80 g dried fish maw, soaked in water for a few hours to soften

2 slices ginger

1 can abalone, reserve 200 ml soaking liquid

400 g dried udon noodles

100 g leafy vegetables of your choice (bok choy, shanghai greens) (optional)

Continuing the Feast
Dried scallops are used in Radish Cake (p 82), Somen with Clams (p 107) and Superior Stock (p 124).

Blanch the chicken bones and chicken breast in a pot of boiling water for 5 minutes to get rid of any scum and impurities. Drain and wash well.

In a stockpot, combine the cleaned chicken parts, dried clam, dried scallops and water. Bring to the boil over low heat and let simmer, uncovered, for 4–5 hours. Skim occasionally to discard any scum.

In the meantime, tear the fish maw into large chunks, then blanch them, along with the ginger slices, in boiling water. The ginger helps get rid of the fishy smell. Drain and set aside.

After the soup has been brewing for 3–4 hours, the flavours from the ingredients will be released. Add the abalone soaking liquid and the fish maw. Let everything boil for 5–10 minutes more.

While that's happening, cook your noodles according to the package instructions and drain them well.

For the greens, you want to add them to your soup at the last possible moment so that they'll retain their vibrancy! So right before serving, toss them in to just cook through.

Place your abalones in a large sieve and let them cook in the soup. Remove and cut into thin slices or leave them chunky — that's completely up to you!

To serve, portion some noodles into a bowl. Arrange some abalone, veggies and fish maw on top, then ladle over the soup. Serve piping hot and slurp up the noodles with all the goodies.

SWEET SOME- THINGS

———

❝ *A party without cake is just a meeting.* ❞

– NORA EPHRON

STICKY PLUM PUDDING WITH BLACK SUGAR TOFFEE SAUCE

This is a play on the classic date-studded sticky pudding cake with its coating of treacle-y and gleaming toffee sauce. In lieu of dates, I use sticky preserved sour plums here and soak them in hot tea to soften. The addition of this tea mixture in the cake batter is what gives it a moist, tender crumb. The toffee sauce is made with black sugar, which is commonly used in many Japanese and Taiwanese sweets, but if you can't find it, you can use dark brown sugar in a pinch. This is best served by warm — microwave or re-heat it — and doused with the sticky toffee sauce. The preserved plum cake base is slightly salty and tart, the perfect counterpart to the rich and dark depths of the black sugar toffee.

MAKES A 23-CM LOAF CAKE

160 g preserved plums, weighed after seeds are removed

170 ml strong black tea

1 tsp baking soda

2 tsp baking powder

155 g plain flour

90 g unsalted butter, at room temperature

80 g black sugar

2 eggs

Pistachios for garnishing, chopped

BLACK SUGAR TOFFEE SAUCE

75 g unsalted butter

150 g black sugar

120 ml heavy cream

1/4 tsp salt

Continuing the Feast
Heavy cream is used in Thai Milk Tea Roll Cake (p 146) and Coconut Panna Cotta (p 149).

First, remove the seeds of your preserved plums. I do this by slicing off chunks of meat from the outside until I reach the seed. You'll want your plums in tiny chunks anyway!

Once you've got 160 g plum meat, set them aside in a small saucepan, along with the tea and baking soda. Bring this mixture to the boil over medium-low heat, boiling for a few minutes to allow the plums to soften. Set aside to cool for 15 minutes.

Using a whisk, mash the plums until you get a black, pulpy sludge. If you prefer a completely smooth mixture, you could use a food processor to blend everything together. Set aside.

Preheat the oven to 175°C. Butter a 23-cm (9-in) loaf pan generously. You could use any other cake pan that's readily available to you, but you will need to adjust the baking time.

Now, for the cake mixture. Whisk the baking powder and flour together, then set aside. You could use a stand mixer to prepare the batter, but it's such a small amount that I prefer to do this by hand, using a whisk and a large mixing bowl. In a separate bowl, beat the butter and sugar together until light and fluffy, about 3–5 minutes. Add the eggs one at a time and beat until the mixture is well emulsified.

Fold in your flour mixture until just combined, then add your plum mixture, being careful not to over-mix. When everything is just combined, scrape the mixture into your prepared loaf pan. Bake for about 35 minutes, until a wooden skewer inserted in the centre comes out clean.

While the cake is baking, get on with the toffee sauce. Place all the ingredients in a saucepan over medium-low heat. Cook until the sugar is melted and a smooth, bubbling sauce forms.

Remove the cake from the oven onto a wire rack. Leave until cool enough to handle before unmoulding. To serve, cut the cake into slices. Douse the cake with the black sugar toffee sauce or drizzle a little on top and serve the sauce on the side. Garnish with chopped pistachios if desired.

MELISSA'S BEST CINNAMON ROLLS

This recipe comes from my amazing baker friend Melissa Joy, whom I met in southern Italy. We hit it off instantly, sharing a passion for pastries, pork fat and books. Melissa is one of the best bakers I have the privilege of knowing — I mean, she makes glazed dried fruit pastry rolls with duck fat pastry! Midway through one of our conversations, cinnamon rolls were mentioned and with a glint in her eyes, she handed me the recipe for these babies, telling me that I HAD to make them. The recipe is straightforward enough but the secret lies in the ratios, which is what makes this basically foolproof. She's tinkered with the recipe to come up with the perfect fat ratio in the dough to ensure a tender end-product. So even if you're utterly clueless about the intricate workings of bread baking, this recipe will still work. This bread dough is as forgiving as your grandma.

MAKES 8–10 ROLLS

DOUGH

400 g plain flour

200 ml milk

1 1/2 tsp instant yeast

65 g white sugar

60 g unsalted butter, melted

1 egg yolk

3/4 tsp salt

CINNAMON SUGAR

80 g light brown sugar

1 1/2 Tbsp ground cinnamon

75 g unsalted butter

CREAM CHEESE FROSTING

250 g cream cheese, softened

30 g unsalted butter, softened

30 g condensed milk

40 g icing sugar

Continuing the Feast
Condensed milk is used in Thai Milk Tea Roll Cake (p 146) and Ginger Milk Pudding (p 151).

To make the bread dough, place all the ingredients in a large mixing bowl. Using a stand mixer with a hook attachment, mix and knead over medium-low speed (about speed 3 or 4) for 5–6 minutes until everything comes together and forms a smooth dough. When poked with a finger, it should spring back lightly.

Pull the rough edges of the dough down and tuck them underneath to form a ball. Cover the mixing bowl with cling film or a tea towel and leave to rise until doubled in volume, about 1–1.5 hours.

Before you begin rolling out the dough, prepare the cinnamon sugar. Mix the sugar and cinnamon together in a bowl. Let the butter stand at room temperature to soften.

Transfer the dough that's doubled in size onto a clean work surface. You can choose to lightly flour the work surface and a rolling pin, but you can get away without doing so. Gently press and lightly flatten the dough into a rectangle. Using a rolling pin, roll out the dough into a 40 x 25-cm rectangle, with the length parallel to you. If you find that the dough springs back or is difficult to roll, leave it alone for 5–10 minutes before trying again. It should roll out quite easily now.

Spread the softened butter evenly on the dough and scatter the cinnamon sugar on top.

Roll the dough along its length away from you to form a long log. Keep tucking the dough as you roll to make sure it's snug. When you've reached the other end, pinch the two edges together to seal the log. You can also moisten them with a little water to help with the sealing.

Turn the log so that the sealed edge sits against the work surface. Cut into log into 8–10 equal rolls.

Generously butter an 8-in (20-cm) round or square baking pan and arrange the rolls in it with the spiral side up. Cover with a tea towel and leave to rise until doubled in size, about 1 hour or so.

Alternatively, leave to proof overnight in the refrigerator and pop them into the oven the next morning for freshly baked cinnamon rolls.

To bake, preheat the oven to 175°C. Bake for 20–25 minutes until golden brown. Remove and set aside to cool while you prepare the cream cheese frosting.

Using a spatula, mash the cream cheese and butter together until combined. Add the condensed milk and icing sugar and whisk together until it takes on more volume. Taste and adjust the sweetness as desired.

Slather the frosting on top of the cinnamon buns and devour while everything's still sticky, gooey and warm.

BROWN BUTTER COCONUT SUGAR MADELEINES

Ah, browned butter, an ingredient that's already divine on its own. We jazz it up even more by combining this nutty aromatic liquid with some vanilla and coconut sugar for these madeleines. The result is a madeleine with an edge — no Plain Jane around here; she's gone for a makeover! To get the requisite hump, rest the madeleine batter in the fridge for at least a couple of hours before baking. Then, a quick blast in a hot oven and you'll have those beautifully humped little tea cakes out in no time for your tea or coffee break.

MAKES ABOUT 16 MINI TEA CAKES

100 g salted butter

2 eggs

65 g coconut sugar

1 tsp vanilla extract or vanilla bean paste

1 Tbsp honey

90 g cake flour

1 tsp baking powder

1/4 tsp baking soda

1 Tbsp rum or whiskey or full-fat milk

Continuing the Feast

Salted butter is used in French Beans Amandine (p 27) and Milk Chocolate Chunk Shortbread (p 144).

Coconut sugar is used in Milk Chocolate Chunk Shortbread (p 144) and Coconut Panna Cotta (p 149).

We'll begin with browning the butter. Heat the butter in a small saucepan over low heat. First, it'll start sizzling and spitting, then its fiery temper will start to cool down as it foams up. You'll notice the colour beneath the foam turning amber as your kitchen is filled with a butterscotch-ey aroma. That's when you know the butter is browned. Pour the browned butter into a cool bowl and set aside.

Generously grease a madeleine pan with softened butter or a baking spray. You can also use any baking pan with mini moulds that you have.

In a large mixing bowl, whisk the eggs, sugar and vanilla extract together for about 5 minutes until foamy and increased in volume. When the whisk is lifted, the mixture should leave voluptuous trails on the batter's surface. Whisk in the honey.

Now's the time to sift in the flour, baking powder and baking soda. Using a spatula, mix until just combined, then fold in the brown butter and rum.

Scoop 2 tablespoonfuls of batter into each mould and leave to rest, uncovered, in the refrigerator for at least a couple of hours before baking.

To bake, preheat the oven to 220°C for 10 minutes. Place the madeleine pan in the oven, reduce the heat to 200°C and bake for 5–8 minutes. Allow the madeleines to cool before unmoulding.

Dust with icing sugar if desired. Serve with cold milk or a cup of coffee or tea!

MILK CHOCOLATE CHUNK
SHORTBREAD WITH COCONUT SUGAR

These highly addictive cookies have a crisp yet tender crumb and are redolent with the scent of butterscotch that makes cookies so universally appealing. The coconut sugar here really amps up that caramel aroma. You can find this sugar, which is coarser than the usual granulated sugar, at health food stores or at Thai supermarkets (it might be shelved in the health food section because it's lower on the glycemic index). Feel free to mix this up by substituting the milk chocolate with dark chocolate or adding cocoa nibs or chopped toasted almonds.

MAKES 18-24 COOKIES, DEPENDING ON HOW YOU PORTION THEM

250 g salted butter, at room temperature

75 g white sugar

45 g coconut sugar

250 g plain flour

35 g cornstarch

150 g milk chocolate, chopped into chunks

Continuing the Feast

Salted butter is used in French Beans Amandine (p 27) and Brown Butter Coconut Sugar Madeleines (p 143).

Coconut sugar is used in Brown Butter Coconut Sugar Madeleines (p 143) and Coconut Panna Cotta (p 149).

In an electric mixer with a whisk attachment or a large mixing bowl, whisk the butter, white sugar and coconut sugar together. Beat for 5–10 minutes until the mixture is light and fluffy.

Fold in the flour and cornstarch until about three-quarters incorporated. You should still see some streaks of flour in the batter. Tip in your milk chocolate chunks and continue mixing until just combined, then stop right there. Go no further, otherwise your shortbread will not be short; they will be tough, dense pucks.

Turn half the dough out onto a work surface lined with cling film. Shape into a log and cover with the cling film. Repeat to shape and cover the other half. Refrigerate the dough logs for a couple of hours or overnight until they are firm.

To bake, preheat the oven to 175°C and line a baking tray.

Cut the logs into 1-cm thick rounds and arrange on the prepared baking tray. Bake for 10–12 minutes until lightly golden brown.

Remove the baking tray onto a wire rack and leave to cool slightly. Enjoy with a glass of cold milk!

THAI MILK TEA ROLL CAKE

Soft and fluffy tea-flavoured sponge cake envelopes a filling of cream that's been infused with Thai tea leaves and whipped into a heavenly delight. To get the tea-cream, steep the tea leaves in heavy cream until it turns a reddish, pale brown hue. For this tender sponge cake, we'll separate the egg whites from the yolks and whisk them separately. This gives the roll its cottony soft texture.

MAKES A 23-CM ROLL CAKE

80 ml tea, from steeping 2 Thai tea bags in 100 ml hot water

3 eggs

100 g white sugar

65 g cake flour

1/2 tsp baking powder

35 ml canola oil

1/4 tsp cream of tartar

CREAM

220 ml heavy cream

4 Thai teabags

3 Tbsp condensed milk, or more to taste

Start with steeping the tea in the cream. Place the heavy cream and teabags in a saucepan over medium heat and bring to the boil. Remove from heat and leave the tea for 30 minutes to steep and cool. When the cream is sufficiently cooled, squeeze the teabags to extract as much flavour as possible before discarding them. Cover and chill the cream in the refrigerator for a couple of hours or overnight.

Moving on to the sponge cake, prepare the tea and let it come to room temperature. Preheat the oven to 175°C. Line a 23-cm (9-in) sheet pan.

Separate the egg whites from the egg yolks. Place the yolks and 60 g sugar in a large mixing bowl. Using an electric mixer with a whisk attachment, whisk at medium speed until the mixture is light, about 1 minute or so. Add the flour, baking powder, oil and cooled tea. Whisk to combine everything into a smooth, pale brown batter.

In a separate mixing bowl, whisk the egg whites and cream of tartar, beginning at low speed and gradually increasing the speed. Add 40 g sugar gradually and whisk until medium peaks form. The egg whites should be glossy and just firm enough to hold their shape on an upside-down whisk.

Using a spatula, fold the egg whites into the yolk batter until just combined. Be very careful not to over-mix this. Transfer the batter onto the prepared sheet pan and smooth it out gently and evenly. Bake for 8–10 minutes, until the sponge cake is puffed up and a nice tan colour.

Remove from the oven and leave to cool for 5 minutes. While the sponge is still warm, peel the sponge cake off from the parchment paper and roll it up into a log. This helps to better set its log shape. Leave on a wire rack to cool to room temperature.

Continuing the Feast

Condensed milk is used in Cinnamon Rolls (p 140) and Ginger Milk Pudding (p 151).

Heavy cream is used in Sticky Plum Pudding (p 138) and Coconut Panna Cotta (p 149).

Return to the chilled tea-infused cream. Add the condensed milk to the cream and whisk until stiff peaks form. If the mixture is a little thin, let it chill in the refrigerator to firm up.

Unroll the sponge cake and spread a thick, even layer of cream on top. Roll up the sponge into a log, wrap in cling film and refrigerate for a couple of hours before slicing. Enjoy this light and refreshing roll cake at tea time!

COCONUT PANNA COTTA WITH LIME CURD AND MANGO

This is a contribution from the doyenne of desserts, Tish Boyle. Anyone who has read *The Cake Book* or *Flavorful* (incidentally, I contributed a recipe to that book!) will know how exacting and passionate about desserts Tish is. I have never followed a recipe of hers that didn't turn out well. When I approached her, Tish was so game for the challenge of coming up with a dessert that incorporates Asian ingredients and here, she's set out to combine some of Thailand's most refreshing flavours. She says, "This dessert is a dance of intense acidity and subtle sweetness. The bottom layer is a sweet coconut panna cotta, and it's topped with a tangy kaffir lime curd. Sweet, fresh mango chunks and a crunchy macadamia-coconut streusel round out this celebration of flavours."

SERVES 6

1 mango, peeled and cut into cubes

6 sprigs cilantro

COCONUT PANNA COTTA

2 sheets gelatine, soaked in iced water for 10 minutes

240 ml coconut cream

35 g white sugar

1/4 tsp salt

LIME CURD

285 g white sugar

160 ml lime juice

Zest of 2 limes

6 kaffir lime leaves

90 g unsalted butter

2 eggs

4 egg yolks

160 g heavy cream

CRUMBLE

40 g plain flour

40 g coconut sugar

35 g desiccated coconut

30 g salted macadamia nuts, roughly chopped

55 g unsalted butter, at room temperature

Continuing the Feast

Coconut sugar is used in Brown Butter Coconut Sugar Madeleines (p 143) and Milk Chocolate Chunk Shortbread (p 144).

Heavy cream is used in Sticky Plum Pudding (p 138) and Thai Milk Tea Roll Cake (p 146).

Desiccated coconut is used in Sam's Chicken Satay (p 54) and Thai Steak Salad (p 60).

Make the panna cotta. While the gelatine sheets are soaking, heat the coconut cream, sugar and salt over low heat. When the mixture comes to a boil, squeeze the gelatine sheets to remove the excess water before adding them to the saucepan. Stir until they dissolve, then remove from heat and portion equally into 6 serving glasses. Leave to cool to room temperature before chilling to set.

Make the lime curd. In a medium saucepan, whisk together 150 g sugar, lime juice, lime zest, lime leaves and butter until combined. Bring the mixture to the boil over medium-high heat.

In a medium bowl, whisk together 135 g sugar, eggs and egg yolks. Slowly pour half of the hot lime mixture into the eggs, whisking constantly. Pour the mixture into the saucepan, whisking as you go, and reduce the heat to medium-low. Stirring constantly with a heatproof spatula, cook until thickened, about 2–3 minutes. Remove from heat and strain through a fine-mesh sieve into a container. Cover, ensuring the cling film comes in direct contact with the mixture's surface, and chill until set, at least 2 hours.

Using an electric mixer with a whisk attachment (or a hand whisk, if you're feeling peppy), whisk the cream until medium peaks form. Gently fold the cream into the chilled lime mixture.

Preheat the oven to 175°C and line a baking tray.

Combine all the crumble ingredients in a bowl and mix until the butter is incorporated and the mixture resembles coarse crumbs. Spread on the prepared baking tray and bake until golden, about 10 minutes. Toss using a spatula and leave to cool completely.

Spoon 3 tablespoonfuls of the crumble on top of the panna cotta in each glass. Set leftover crumble aside. Spoon or pipe the lime curd over, top with some diced mango, then cover each glass and refrigerate for at least 1 hour. Right before serving, top each one with some of the remaining crumble and a sprig of cilantro.

We dipped our spoons into the most ethereal, softly set curd, its sweet milkiness offset by the spicy warmth of old ginger.

GINGER MILK PUDDING

My friend Zoe and I were strolling around Causeway Bay in Hong Kong when we chanced upon this shop called Yee Shun Milk Company. Our interests piqued, we went inside and found ourselves in a no-frills dessert restaurant with many bowls of milk pudding neatly stacked away in utilitarian steel drawers. Of course, we had to get ourselves some pudding. We dipped our spoons into the most ethereal, softly set curd, its sweet milkiness offset by the spicy warmth of old ginger.

This recipe is my approximation of that beautiful dessert. The intriguing part of this recipe is the setting agent — it's not your usual gelatine or agar; we're using ginger here. To be more specific, we're using old ginger as it has an enzyme that sets the protein in milk, creating that delicate pudding-like texture.

SERVES 2

1 large knob old ginger, about 10–12 cm in length

200 ml full-fat milk

25 g condensed milk

$1/4$ tsp vanilla extract (optional)

Continuing the Feast
Condensed milk is used in Cinnamon Rolls (p 140) and Thai Milk Tea Roll Cake (p 146).

Notes

You must use the old, wrinkly type of mature ginger for this. They've got rougher skins. Young ginger doesn't have the particular enzyme required to set the milk to pudding.

You can choose to reduce or increase the amount of ginger in the recipe. Do note that too little ginger won't set the curds. If you choose to increase the amount of ginger, you might have to increase the level of sweetness to counteract the ginger's slight bitterness.

Don't let the ginger juice sit out for too long or its setting prowess will be gone.

Give the ginger juice a good stir before portioning it into the bowls.

We'll begin with extracting ginger juice. Using a mortar and pestle, pound the ginger into a pulpy mass and press it against a fine-mesh sieve to extract the ginger juice, about 5 teaspoonfuls. You can also use a blender, food processor or grater. I find the most efficient way is to use a mortar and pestle, as grating takes way longer than just smashing it into a pulp.

Prepare 2 serving bowls. Give the ginger juice a good stir and portion 2 teaspoonfuls into each serving bowl. For a spicier, gingery flavour, put $2^1/2$ teaspoonfuls in each bowl. Set aside.

Heat the milk, condensed milk and vanilla extract, if using, in a saucepan over low heat until the mixture is 70°C. Use a thermometer here as the enzymes won't work to set the curd at a higher or lower temperature.

Once the milk mixture is at the right temperature, remove from heat and divide equally into the bowls with the ginger juice. Resist the urge to do anything to it from now on. Just let it sit there for 5–10 minutes, allowing the ginger to work its magic.

Once the mixture has set, you have your magical ginger custard. You can either serve it immediately or chill overnight so you can enjoy it cold the next day.

―――――

*"Travelling — it leaves you speechless,
then turns you into a storyteller."*

― IBN BATTUTA